OUT OF THE STORM

To the saints at All Saints,
Little Shelford, 1997–2004

OUT OF THE STORM

Grappling with God in the book of Job

Christopher Ash

Inter-Varsity Press
Norton Street, Nottingham NG7 3HR, England
Email: ivp@ivpbooks.com
Website: www.ivpbooks.com

First published 2004
Reprinted 2009

British Library Cataloguing in Publication Data
A catalogue record for this book is available from the British Library.

ISBN 978-1-84474-056-7

Set in Monotype Dante 10.5/13pt
Typeset in Great Britain by Servis Filmsetting Ltd, Manchester
Printed and bound in Great Britain by Ashford Colour Press Ltd, Gosport, Hampshire

Inter-Varsity Press publishes Christian books that are true to the Bible and that
communicate the gospel, develop discipleship and strenthen the church for its mission
in the world.
Inter-Varsity Press is closely linked with the Universities and Colleges Christian
Fellowship, a student movement connecting Christian Unions in universities and
colleges throughout Great Britain, and a member movement of the International
Fellowship of Evangelical Students. Website: www.uccf.org.uk

Contents

Preface   7

Outline and structure of the book of Job   9

1. What is the book of Job about?   11

2. Do we live in a well-run world? (Job 1:1 – 2:10)   16

3. Weep with those who weep (Job 2:11 – 3:26)   24

4. What not to say to the suffering believer (Job 4 – 27)   35

5. Two marks of a real believer (Job 4 – 27)   47

6. Is God for me or against me? (Job 19)   55

7. Why will God not answer my question? (Job 28)   64

8. Why justification matters desperately (Job 29 – 31)   75

9. A surprising new voice (Job 32 – 37)   81

10. The God who is God (Job 38:1 – 42:6)   89

11. The end comes at the end (Job 42:7–17)   100

Postscript: So what is the book of Job about?   109

Preface

This book is not a treatment of a topic, whether the topic of suffering or of anything else. It is a study of the Bible book of Job. I want you to venture into the book of Job, to read, meditate, explore and pray this profound Bible book into your bloodstream. If you have never done so, my prayer is that this short study will help you find a way in. If you have ventured in but got bogged down and confused, I hope this introduction will signpost the main roads.

Job is a neglected treasure of the Christian life. It has spawned an enormous outpouring of scholarly work, and yet few Christians know quite where to start in appropriating its message for themselves.

My own interest in Job was first stirred by Robert Fyall's excellent and provocatively entitled book, *How Does God Treat his Friends?* (Christian Focus, 1995). I have also been helped by technical commentaries, notably those of John E. Hartley, *The Book of Job*, New International Commentary on the Old Testament (Grand Rapids, Mich.: Eerdmans, 1988), and Norman C. Habel, *The Book of Job* (Philadelphia: Westminster Press, 1985), and by Robert Fyall's scholarly study, *Now my Eyes Have Seen you* (Apollos, 2002). To Fyall in particular my debt is considerable, both in exegesis and in illustrative material.

This book began as a series of seven sermons preached in the evening services at All Saints, Little Shelford, while I was their pastor.

I have since taught Job on the Cornhill Training Course, where there was time to go into much more detail, and to students at Cambridge University in Christian Union meetings. I am grateful for these opportunities and to all who have given helpful comments and feedback. It will be obvious that this short study is no substitute for a full commentary and makes no pretence at comprehensiveness. We shall focus only on the main roads through Job. The thoughtful reader will have all sorts of questions to follow up with deeper study. But if I can open a way in for some believers, I shall have fulfilled my purpose.

Christopher Ash
Little Shelford, Cambridge
March 2004

Outline and structure of the book of Job

PART 1. JOB AND WHAT HAPPENED TO HIM

Introducing Job   1:1–5
What happened to Job   1:6 – 2:10

PART 2. JOB'S FRIENDS AND THEIR 'CONVERSATIONS' WITH JOB

Introducing Job's three friends   2:11–13
Speeches by Job and his friends   3:1 – 27:23

Job's 1st lament (3)

1st cycle of speeches
Eliphaz (4 – 5)   Job (6 – 7)
Bildad (8)   Job (9 – 10)
Zophar (11)   Job (12 – 14)

2nd cycle of speeches
Eliphaz (15)   Job (16 – 17)
Bildad (18)   Job (19)
Zophar (20)   Job (21)

3rd cycle of speeches (interrupted)
Eliphaz (22)   Job (23 – 24)
Bildad (25)   Job (26 – 27)

Poem about wisdom   28:1–28
Job's final defence   29:1 – 31:40

PART 3. THE ANSWERS TO JOB

Introducing Elihu   32:1–5
Elihu's answers   32:6 – 37:24
The Lord's first answer and Job's response   38:1 – 40:5
The Lord's second answer and Job's response   40:6 – 42:6
Conclusion   42:7–17

1. What is the book of Job about?

This book began as a sermon series on the book of Job. Twelve days before the first sermon, on 14 January 2003, Detective Constable Stephen Oake was stabbed and killed in Manchester. Why? He was an upright man, a faithful husband and a loving father. What is more, he was a Christian, a committed member of his church, where he sometimes used to preach. The newspapers reported the moving statement by his father, Robin Oake, a former chairman of the Christian Police Association: how he said through his tears that he was praying for the man who had killed his son. They told of the quiet dignity of his widow, Lesley. They showed the happy family snapshots with his teenage son Christopher and daughters Rebecca and Corinne.

So why was *he* killed? Does this not make us angry? After all, if we are going to be honest, we have to admit that there were others who deserved to die more than him. Perhaps there was a corrupt policeman somewhere, who had unjustly put innocent people in prison, or a crooked policeman who had taken bribes. Or perhaps there was another policeman who was carrying on an affair with his neighbour's wife. If one of those had been killed, we might have said that, although we were sad, at least there would have appeared to be some moral logic to this death. But this family are, dare we say it, good people. Not sinless, of course, but believers living upright lives. So why was this pointless and terrible loss inflicted on *them*?

We need to be honest and face the kind of world we live in. Why does God allow these things? Why does he do nothing to put these things right? And why, on the other hand, do people who could not care less about God and justice thrive? Here in contemporary idiom is the angry voice of an honest man from long ago, who also struggled with these same injustices:

> Why do the wicked have it so good,
> live to a ripe old age and get rich?
> They get to see their children succeed,
> get to watch and enjoy their grandchildren.
> Their homes are peaceful and free from fear;
> they never experience God's disciplining rod.
> Their bulls breed with great vigour
> and their calves calve without fail.
> They send out their children to play
> and watch them frolic like spring lambs.
> They make music with fiddles and flutes,
> have good times singing and dancing.
> They have a long life on easy street,
> and die painlessly in their sleep![1]

'Let's be honest,' Job says. 'Let's have no more of this pious make-believe that it goes well for good people and badly for bad people. You look around the world and it's simply not true. By and large people who could not care about God live happier, longer lives with less suffering than do believers. Why? What kind of God might it be who runs a world like this?'

We face hard questions like this in the book of Job. But there are two ways to ask these questions. We may ask them as 'armchair questions' or we may ask them as 'wheelchair questions'. We ask them as 'armchair questions' if we ourselves are remote from suffering. As Shakespeare said, 'He jests at scars that never felt a wound.'[2] The troubled Jesuit poet Gerard Manley Hopkins wrote eloquently and almost bitterly:

O the mind, mind has mountains; cliffs of fall
Frightful, sheer, no-man fathomed. Hold them cheap
May who ne'er hung there . . .[3]

We grapple with God with 'wheelchair questions' when we do not
hold this terror cheap, when we ourselves or those we love are suffering. Job asks the 'wheelchair questions'.

Every pastor knows that behind most front doors lies pain, often
hidden, sometimes long-drawn-out, sometimes very deep. I was dis-
cussing how to preach a passage from Job with four fellow ministers,
when I looked around at the others. For a moment I lost my concentration on the text as I realized that one of them, some years before,
had lost his wife in a car accident in their first year of marriage. The
second was bringing up a seriously handicapped daughter. The third
had broken his neck and come within 2 mm of total paralysis or
death six years previously. And the fourth had undergone repeated
radical surgery, which had changed his life. As my concentration
returned to the text of Job, I thought, 'This book is not merely academic: it is both about and for people who know suffering.'

Job is a fireball book. It is a staggeringly honest book. It is a book
that knows what people actually say and think – and not just what
they say publicly in church. It knows what people say behind closed
doors and in whispers; and it knows what we say in our tears. It is not
merely an academic book. If we listen to it with any care, it will
touch, trouble and unsettle us at a deep level.

Before we launch into the book, let me make two introductory
points.

Job is a very long book

Job is 42 chapters long. We may consider that rather an obvious
observation, but the point is this: in his wisdom God has given us a
very long book. He has done so for a reason. It is easy just to preach
the beginning and the end, and to skip rather quickly over the
endless arguments in between as if it would not much matter if they
were not there. But God has put them there.

Why? Well, just maybe because when the suffering question and the 'Where is God?' question and the 'What kind of God?' question are asked from the wheelchair, they cannot be answered on a post-card. If we ask, 'What kind of God allows this kind of world?', God gives us a 42-chapter book. Far from saying, 'Well, the message of Job may be summarized on a postcard and here it is,' he says, 'Come with me on a journey, a journey that will take time. There is no instant answer – take a spoonful of Job, add boiling water and you'll know the answer.' Job cannot be distilled. It is a narrative with a slow pace (after the frenetic beginning) and long delays. Why? Because there is no instant working through grief, no quick fix to pain, no message of Job in a nutshell. God has given us a 42-chapter journey with no satis-factory bypass.

Indeed, if this short study is treated as an *alternative* to reading the text of Job, it will be like reading a guide book to a foreign country as a substitute for actually visiting it, rather than as a preparation and accompaniment. This study is to help us read the book of Job itself. For we must read it, and read it at length and at leisure.

This is just a short introductory study. But it may be better by a short introduction to tempt you into the book and open up the book to a lifetime of study, than by a forbiddingly long tome to slam the door in your faces. When I was sent to Rome some years ago on busi-ness, I managed during one weekend to scrape together just 24 hours to visit Florence. It seemed in some ways almost insulting to the riches of the Uffizi Gallery alone to give just one day to it. But it was better than nothing, and it gave me the desire to go back and explore further. If this book achieves that, it will have been worthwhile.

Most of Job is poetry

About 95% of the book of Job is poetry. Chapters 1 and 2, the start of chapter 32, and part of chapter 42 are prose. All the rest is poetry. But so what? Well, so quite a lot. For poetry does not speak to us in the same way as prose. For poems, says J. I. Packer, 'are always a personal "take" on something, communicating not just from head to head but from heart to heart'.[4] A poem can often touch, move and unsettle us in ways that prose cannot. Job is a blend of the affective (touching our feelings) and the cognitive (addressing our minds). And poetry is particularly suited to this balanced address to the whole person. But poetry does not lend itself to summing up in tidy propositions, bullet points, neat systems and well-swept answers. Poetry grapples with our emotions, wills and sensitivities. We cannot just sum up a poem in a bald statement; we need to let a poem get to work on us, to immerse ourselves in it.

It is just so with Job. We shall be immersed in the poetry of Job. As we enter it we must not expect tidy systematic points to note down and then think we've 'done' Job, as a one-day tourist might 'do' Florence. Job is to be lived in and not just studied. So during this study let us read the book of Job itself, read it out loud, mull it over, absorb it, wonder, be unsettled and meditate. And let God get to work on us through this great Bible book.

Notes

1. From *The Message* paraphrase of Job 21 (Eugene H. Patterson, NavPress 1996).
2. *Romeo and Juliet*, Act II, Scene 2.
3. Gerard Manley Hopkins, Sonnet 41.
4. Quoted from Gaius Davies, *Genius, Grief and Grace* (Christian Focus, 2001), p. 8.

2 Do we live in a well-run world? (Job 1:1 – 2:10)

The scene is set (1:1–5)

There was a man in the land of Uz whose name was Job, and that man was blameless and upright, one who feared God and turned away from evil. (1:1)

Job was 'healthy, wealthy and wise'. This is what we would expect in a well-run world: that one who is wise will as a consequence be healthy and wealthy. After all, to be wise – in the Bible sense – means to fear and honour the living God (as human beings ought in their religion) and to turn away from wrongdoing (as human beings ought in their morality). And any self-respecting god who claims to be both fair and in control is surely bound to reward such a person with wealth and health. To do otherwise would be either unfair or evidence of weakness. Likewise we may expect to meet others who are 'sick, poor and wicked', their wickedness leading inevitably to illness and destitution.

We do not know where Job lived. (No-one knows where Uz was, except that it does not seem to have been anywhere in Israel.) We do not know when he lived (except that it feels like a very long time ago). He could be almost anybody, were it not for what the storyteller tells us in the first verse: that Job is a real believer in the living God. He *fears God*, bowing down before him in wonder, love and awe, recognizing that God alone is the Creator to whom he and his world owe their entire existence. And as a mark of true worship, he *turns away from evil*; his life from day to day being marked by repentance and faith. In Job 28 there is a poem about wisdom. The conclusion (28:28) is that wisdom is to *fear God* and *turn away from evil*; which is precisely what we are told about Job in the first verse of the book. Job is, in the deepest biblical sense, a wise man. That is to say, he is a believer, a true worshipper. He is *blameless*, which does not mean he is perfect, but rather that he has personal integrity; his life is of a piece; what he says with his lips in spoken worship he lives with his life in whole-body worship. 'Blameless' is the word translated 'sincerity' in Joshua 24:14 (*Now therefore fear the* LORD *and serve him in sincerity . . .*). And he is *upright*, which means both loyal to God and straight in his dealings with others. It seems from the passing allusions to him in Ezekiel 14:14, 20 that Job's righteousness was legendary. Here before us at the start of the story is the true believer par excellence, a man who walks before God with a clear conscience, his sins confessed and forgiven, his life showing all the marks of a worshipper.

And if we believe that this world is ordered by a fair God, we are not at all surprised by the blessing that follows:

> There were born to him seven sons and three daughters. He possessed 7,000 sheep, 3,000 camels, 500 yoke of oxen, and 500 female donkeys, and very many servants, so that this man was the greatest of all the people of the east. His sons used to go and hold a feast in the house of each one on his day, and they would send and invite their three sisters to eat and drink with them. And when the days of the feast had run their course, Job would send and consecrate them, and he would rise early in the morning and offer burnt offerings according to the number of them all. For Job said, 'It may be that my children have sinned, and cursed God in their hearts.' Thus Job did continually. (Job 1:2–5)

We meet here a large, harmonious family filled with godly celebration and joy, and material wealth beyond the wildest dreams of the wicked. And yet (verse 5) amid this wonderful blessing Job maintains his godliness; he is watchful in prayer, ever concerned as his highest priority in life to keep himself and his family in right relationship with God. So here he is, a paragon of virtue and showered with blessings. What a feel-good start to a happy story!

And now the horrifying surprise. Four sharp, quick, alternating scenes, the first three signalled by *Now there was a day . . .* We may picture them dramatized on a stage. Stage left, the Lord's council chamber; stage right, Job's land. As we walk through this staccato drama, let us watch for the four salient features or markers our storyteller wants to fix in our minds at the outset of our journey. It is vital for us to be absolutely clear about these; otherwise we shall be hopelessly confused when we get into the body of the book. And the storyteller also poses a big question.

- Marker 1: Job really is blameless
- Marker 2: Satan has real influence
- Marker 3: The Lord is absolutely supreme
- Marker 4: The Lord gives terrible permissions
- Question: Will Job prove to be a real believer?

Scene 1: The Lord's council chamber (1:6–12)

Lights up, stage left. We are in the heavenly council chamber. This is a way of picturing the spiritual government of the world that we find, for example, in Psalm 82:1. We find something similar in 1 Kings 22:19–22. The Lord is in the chair. (When our English translations print 'LORD', this translates the Hebrew word 'Yahweh', the God of Israel, of the Bible and of the whole world.) The *sons of God* (or 'angels', NIV) are the spiritual beings entrusted with power under the Lord in the universe. They are taking their seats for a Cabinet meeting. This Bible imagery helps us to recognize that we live in a world in which all manner of spiritual and very real powers and authorities are at work, and yet all of them are subject to the sovereign God.

Among the spiritual beings is *Satan*, or, more literally, 'the Satan'; for this is a title rather than a personal name. He is the enemy, the adversary, the accuser, a kind of public prosecutor. It seems to be his job to patrol the earth looking for sin. It is not clear at this stage whose enemy he is. The Lord asks Satan where he has come from (verse 7). This may be a hostile question, implying that Satan is gate-crashing the meeting or that his doings are the subject of the Lord's suspicion. Or it may be a routine enquiry: 'Now, Mr Satan, time for your report.'

'Oh,' he says, 'just doing stuff, here and there, the usual . . .'

'And what did you find?' For the Lord is always on the lookout for real believers, men and women with integrity who will love and worship him as they ought. Maybe Satan shrugs as if to imply he has not found any real worshippers, with the further implication that perhaps the Chairman of the Council is not the best person to be in charge, since he has no real adherents on earth.

And so the Lord picks up this implicit challenge: *Have you noticed my servant Job?* The title *my servant* is a mark of honour and special closeness to God, used in the Bible of Abraham, Isaac, Jacob, Moses and the prophets. It is used supremely of the 'servant' of the Lord in Isaiah 42:1 and the other so-called 'Servant Songs' in Isaiah, an utterly blameless figure who also suffers terribly in spite of – or because of? – his righteousness.

'Job seems pretty special to me,' says the Lord: 'Blameless, upright, fearing God and turning away from evil. So what do you make of him?' (verse 8, echoing verse 1). This challenge in 1:8 is the main-spring from which unwinds the whole terrible drama of the book. 'Here, it seems to me', says God, 'is a true worshipper. Now what are you going to do about *that*?'

Well, Satan is not impressed. 'What, him a true worshipper?! Well, hardly, Your Majesty. Anyone would have the outward show of being a believer if he'd been given what Job has been given. You've put a protective hedge around him. He's never suffered any loss. He's a fair-weather believer, if you ask me. But if you want publicly, before all these other spiritual beings, to prove this believer is a real one, then you'll have to show them the genuineness of his faith.[1] And you can only do that when he suffers loss. Then I think we'll all see that his is not real worship. Take away what he has and he'll curse you; and then we'll see revealed a heart just like all the others on earth. You see, Your Majesty, your world is completely ruined. Not a believer in sight. Shame, isn't it?' We can hear the sneer in his voice.

And the shocking thing is that the Lord says yes: 'You've asked me to stretch out my hand [verse 11]. Why don't you do it for me and stretch out yours? Take away what he has. But don't touch the man himself.'

Now this permission is shocking. The storyteller has told us in verse 1 that Job is blameless. God himself has reiterated this in verse 8. He does not deserve to suffer as he is about to do. This suffering is not a punishment for any unforgiven sin in his life. That is the first shock. Further, this permission is given by a God who does not have to give it. God is sovereign. Satan is at best a member of God's council, not a rival emperor. He is, as Luther put it, 'God's Satan'. And yet this God who is in control says to Satan, 'Off you go and make Job suffer loss.'

We ought to be shocked by that. The Auschwitz survivor Harold Kushner called his bestselling book *When Bad Things Happen to Good People*. In this book Kushner 'solves' the problem of suffering essentially by saying that God is doing his best and it is not his fault if he does not manage to eliminate suffering. It is not as if he is all-powerful, after all. This is a common 'solution' today. In Christian circles it surfaces in what is sometimes called 'openness theism'. This says essentially that while God is powerful and knows the past, he does not know the future, let alone decide exactly what the future contains. No, he is more like a chess grandmaster, expert at the game, but never quite sure what the opposition may throw at him, and we can never be quite sure he will win. But we may be sure he is doing his best.

The book of Job will not allow that, any more than the rest of the Bible will. No, without question God is in control. Satan has to ask permission, and what Satan then does cannot go one millimetre beyond the permission he has been given. And the scandal is that the supreme God does give permission to Satan to cause God's blameless servant to suffer. And suffer he does.

Scene 2: Job's land (1:13–22)

Lights up, stage right. In terrifying staccato succession Job is stabbed by woe after woe. His oxen and donkeys are stolen and his servants killed by war, terrorism or violent crime (verses 14–15). Before he has time to come to terms with this loss, another messenger tells him some natural disaster has killed his sheep and shepherds (verse 16). Likewise (verse 17) the camels by violent men. And then, as if these three hammer blows were not enough, the numbing news of the death of his children in a freak storm (verses 18–19). Human evil, then 'natural' disaster, then human evil and then 'natural' disaster.

Not surprisingly (verse 20), Job is desolate. But (verse 21) he responds with wonderful faith, in words often read at a funeral service. Job's faith seems to be proved genuine (verse 22). Things may be unspeakably painful for him, but they are deeply threatening for Satan, whose whole project of hostility to God is under threat by this man who worships the living God even when he has no blessing to show for it.

But the drama is far from over. The cycle begins again.

Scene 3: The Lord's council chamber (2:1–7a)

Lights up, stage left. The scene closely echoes Scene 1. Again we hear the challenge to Satan (verse 3); again the affirmation of Job's blamelessness (verse 3), with the additional comment that Job *still holds fast his integrity, although you incited me against him to destroy him.* War is being waged, and Job himself is the battleground. 'He's proving to be a real believer, and not just for what blessings he can get out of it, don't you think?' asks the Lord.

But again Satan is unimpressed. 'Pah! We haven't gone nearly far enough. So long as a man has his health he's not really been tested. It's not a big deal to take all his money and make him bury all his children. No, stretch out your hand and take his own health and then he'll curse you.'

And again it's a shock to us. We might expect the Lord to call a halt, to say, 'Enough is enough! The man has suffered more numbing trauma in one terrible sequence than most human beings do in a lifetime.' But he does not call a halt. No, he tells Satan he can go ahead and stretch out his hand against the person of Job himself. The only condition is that he may not kill Job. It is a condition many today wish, and Job himself wishes, had not been imposed. As we shall see, Job's suffering is so intense he longs for death, but cannot find it (3:21).

And so, without even the dramatic pause of *there was a day* we are tumbled straight into Scene 4.

Scene 4: Job's land (2:7b–10)

Satan strikes Job with loathsome physical suffering. He has already made Job's mental, emotional and spiritual life a torture; now he torments his bodily existence so that at no moment of day or night can Job forget his pain. We do not know quite why his wife says what she does (verse 9); maybe she just cannot stand watching him suffer like that; she would not be the first to struggle with the suffering of a loved one and to wish death upon them. But Job will not have it (verse 10): no, he says, to curse God would be foolish. We accept good things from God; we ought to be able to accept trouble as well. And again, as in 1:22, our storyteller ends the scene with an affirmation that Job's faith is holding up (2:10).

It is tempting to think we can skip now to Job 42 and go home feeling good despite our hero's terrible ordeal. For 'all's well that ends well', as we say. But that would be too shallow. For the drama of Job is never simple or superficial. Between Job 2 and Job 42 is an age of agony, perplexity and suffering. If we are to understand that agony we cannot skip those chapters in between.

But as we embark on those long poetic chapters, we need to keep in mind the four clear markers our storyteller has signalled to us, and the big question he has left us with.

- *Marker 1: Job really is blameless.* As the poetry unfolds we shall see Job obstinately maintaining his righteousness. We shall be tempted to doubt him. 'Without this prologue the reader would side with the three comforters, thinking Job to be a demented villain, hostile to God and self-deluded about his own moral virtue.'[2] We need to remember that three times (once by the narrator in 1:1, twice by the Lord in 1:8 and 2:3) we have been clearly told that Job is blameless and upright, that he fears God and turns away from evil.
- *Marker 2: Satan has real influence.* Some operate on a naïve model of spiritual realities in which there is simply one God in control and all human affairs are directly ordained by him. God, if we may put it

like this, is the only spiritual power or reality; all the rest is human and visible. The book of Job signals to us at the start that there are other real, influential, unseen spiritual powers, of whom Satan is one. These powers may be subsidiary to the Lord, but they may not be ignored.

- *Marker 3: The Lord is absolutely supreme.* Alongside Marker 2 we must remember that the Bible gives no encouragement to the idea that God is anything other than all-powerful. The book of Job is no exception. Indeed it is a vital part of its tension and drama that we know at the very start that the living God, the Lord, is the only supreme God. Nothing happens in the universe without his permission.

- *Marker 4: The Lord gives terrible permissions.* We have seen and been shocked by these permissions. We ought never to be other than shocked by them, and never to take them for granted as unexceptionable. For they are horrifying.

- *Question: Will Job prove to be a real believer?* It seems so from 1:22 and 2:10. But if his faith is so simple and genuine, why the need for thirty-nine chapters of highly charged poetry before we reach the conclusion? We must carry this question with us on our journey.

Notes

1. 1 Peter 1:7.
2. John E. Hartley, *The Book of Job*, New International Commentary on the Old Testament (Grand Rapids, Mich.: Eerdmans, 1988), p. 22.

3 Weep with those who weep
(Job 2:11 – 3:26)

After this Job opened his mouth and cursed the day of his birth. (3:1)

In Job 3 we must weep with those who weep (Romans 12:15). When this chapter was preached at All Saints, Little Shelford, we did not sing at all in our evening service. Neither a hymn, nor a song. Although some of us had come to the evening service feeling quite cheerful, our own circumstances full of hope, we needed to weep with one who wept. And so we read together Psalm 137, where the people of God are asked to sing one of the songs of Zion but cannot sing, so deep is their distress. A terribly painful psalm, with its desperate cry for revenge wrung from broken hearts: 'We have seen our young children murdered; we have heard their screams – well, just maybe someone will do that to your children, you torturers, and when they do, good for them!' It is terrible. But that is how they felt. 'We cannot sing. And if you force us to be happy, it will add torment to our misery.' 'Cheer up! Pull yourselves together!' said their tormentors. But they could not.

We listened to the puzzling story of William Cowper, the great Christian poet and hymnwriter. How his life was blighted first by the death of his mother when he was 6; how fifty-three years later when someone sent him a portrait of her, he wrote a moving poem that makes it clear his grief was ever fresh. It included the lines

I heard the bell tolled on thy burial day,
I saw the hearse that bore thee slow away,
And turning from my nursery window, drew
A long, long sigh, and wept a last adieu!

We heard how Cowper's father sent him away to a boarding school where he was cruelly bullied, and probably never recovered in his mind. And how after a two-year engagement his fiancée's father forbad the marriage. How before his conversion he suffered repeated episodes of deep depressive illness. 'I was struck', he wrote, 'with such a dejection of spirits, as none but they who have felt the same, can have the least conception of. Day and night I was upon the rack, lying down in horror, and rising up in despair.'

We listened to how, aged 31, Cowper suffered a catastrophic psychotic breakdown, tried three times to take his own life and was committed to an asylum, what would now be a psychiatric hospital. An evangelical Christian ran this asylum, where six months later Cowper met the Lord Jesus Christ and became his disciple. Describing his conversion he wrote, 'Unless the Almighty arm had been under me, I think I should have died with gratitude and joy. My eyes filled with tears, and my voice choked with transport; I could only look up to heaven in silent fear, overwhelmed with wonder and love.'

It was a wonderful change and a real conversion. And yet on four more occasions in his life he suffered deep depressive illness. And shortly before he died of dropsy (oedema) in 1800 one of the last things he said was, 'I feel unutterable despair.'[1]

And this was a Christian, a real Christian who has bequeathed to the church some of its deepest and greatest hymns. That evening we looked together at his great hymn 'O for a closer walk with God', in which he laments the loss of the blessedness he first knew when he met the Lord Jesus. And how his diagnosis for his despair is that there must be an idol in his life. And if only he can be helped to tear that idol from God's throne in his life, then again his walk will be close with God and calmness and serenity will return to his life. And we considered the possibility that great though that hymn is, and much as it applies to many believers, it may have been written out of a false diagnosis of Cowper's own condition. That is, that his despair might not have had anything to do with a backsliding or a turning away from the worship of the true God. For as we shall see in this chapter, Job's despair was not the result of his backsliding or unforgiven sin.

We listened to Wilfred Owen's haunting poem 'Futility'. Owen laments the futility of the whole created order as he stands by the body of a young man lying dead on the Western Front in World War I.

> Move him into the sun –
> Gently its touch awoke him once,
> At home, whispering of fields unsown.
> Always it woke him, even in France,
> Until this morning and this snow.
> If anything might rouse him now
> The kind old sun will know.
>
> Think how it wakes the seeds, –
> Woke, once, the clays of a cold star.
> Are limbs, so dear-achieved, are sides,
> Full-nerved – still warm – too hard to stir?
> Was it for this the clay grew tall?
> – O what made fatuous sunbeams toil
> To break earth's sleep at all?

We listened also to the unrelieved laments of Psalm 88 and Jeremiah 20:7–18. And then we listened to the lament of Job 3. And then, after the sermon, we went home. It was a sobering evening with one aim: that we might grasp that a real believer may go through blank despair and utter desperation. That a blameless believer, who has not fallen into sin, may go through utter dereliction, and yet at the end be seen to be a real believer. That we might grasp that we ourselves, if we walk closely with Christ, may go through very deep darkness, deeper even perhaps than if we had not walked faithfully in his footsteps. And that as we grasp this sobering truth we may learn to weep with those who weep.

Job 3 is a very important chapter for contemporary Christianity. For there is a version of Christianity around that is shallow, trite, superficial, 'happy clappy' (as they say). It is a kind of Christianity that someone has said, 'would have Jesus singing a chorus at the grave of Lazarus'. We have all met it: easy triumphalism. We sing of God in one song, that 'in his presence our problems disappear', and in another that 'my love just keeps on growing'. Neither was true for Job in chapter 3; and yet he was a real and blameless believer.

I have on my shelf a book about Christians who suffer depression and anxiety; it is called *I'm Not Supposed to Feel Like This*,[2] which is a provocative title. 'It is bad enough that I feel low or anxious', says the Christian. 'But on top of that I feel guilty: for I ought not to feel low, as a Christian. I feel that I ought to be able to cast my cares upon him, for he cares for me (1 Peter 5:7). And yet somehow I can't.'

In Job 1 – 2 we watched this blameless believer suffer heart-rending loss: his possessions ruined, his children killed, his health destroyed. And we listened – as Job could not – to the conversations in heaven that lay behind his loss; between God and Satan, the enemy; and how the Lord gives his terrible permissions to Satan to torture Job. Job is not being punished for his sin. Exactly the reverse: Job suffers precisely because he is conspicuously godly. And he suffers deep deprivation – physical, mental, emotional, social and spiritual loss.

And yet still he shows faith, in two remarkable responses often celebrated in Christian and Jewish history:

- *Naked I came from my mother's womb, and naked shall I return. The* LORD *gave, and the* LORD *has taken away; blessed be the name of the* LORD. (1:21)
- *Shall we receive good from God, and shall we not receive evil?* (2:10)

Both Jewish and Christian piety have wanted to major on Job's faith, which is not surprising, for Job's faith here is stunning. But the danger with our focusing on 1:21 and 2:10 is that we make Job's faith two-dimensional. 'He suffered; he trusted,' we say. 'And so should we. End of story.'

But it is far from the end of the story. For in 3:1 Job curses the day of his birth. And we are brought up short. For Job then goes on lamenting and protesting for chapter after chapter. We must not soften this. We must remember that at the end of the book (Job 42)

God affirms that Job has spoken rightly of him, that Job is God's servant, that Job is a righteous man (who can therefore pray and expect his prayers to be heard). The despair of Job 3 is the authentic experience of a man affirmed by God at the start (1:8; 2:3) and affirmed again by God at the end (42:7). We need to remember that. It is surprising, for Job 3 is a dark chapter.

The visit of Job's friends (2:11–13) draws our attention, paradoxically and poignantly, to the fact that Job is terribly alone.

Job is terribly alone

In 2:8 we see Job alone in his grief. He sits *in the ashes*: on the dump outside the city, where the rubbish is burned, the place Jesus later referred to as Gehenna or Hell. And he sits there alone. His wife appears in 2:9, but only to have an argument. And then in 2:11 three friends hear about his troubles and come *to show him sympathy* (to share his grief) *and comfort him* (to ease his pain). They come from different places; in symbol they are the wisdom of the world gathering to this sufferer.

And as they catch their first glimpse of their old friend they are appalled (2:12). 'Is that Job?!' So thin, so pale, so drawn, so harrowed with pain and grief.' And they weep, tear their clothes and throw dirt on their heads; and they sit with him in silence for seven days and seven nights. It is usual to say that this was the best thing they did. And certainly (as we shall see in Job 4), when they speak they do no good at all. But their silence may not have been as helpful as is often assumed. For the Bible hints that what they do, symbolically – the torn clothes, the dust on the head, the seven days – is what one does in mourning with a corpse. So Joseph mourns seven days for his father Jacob (Genesis 50:10); the city of Ramoth Gilead mourns seven days for King Saul (1 Samuel 31:13). And it may be that their silence is not so much a silence of sympathy as a silence of bankruptcy: they are silent because they have nothing to say. Their friend is as good as dead. In our culture it is as if they call for the hearse and sit by Job with the coffin open and ready. And it is Job who has to break the silence (3:1). For Job is terribly alone.

But whatever the meaning of their silence, the book of Job brings home to us the loneliness of suffering. Sometimes in Scripture there are corporate laments; Psalm 137 is one such. But this is so personal, and Job is so alone. Suffering does that. Even a non-serious illness cuts us off from others; we have to miss out on a family outing, a party or a gathering. There is (in the title of an old play) 'Laughter in the room next door'. And if even light suffering begins to isolate the sufferer, heavy suffering isolates acutely. Even a shared loss is experienced uniquely by a bereft person. When a child dies, the father alone knows what it is to be the father of this dead child; only the mother enters the unique depths of loss as the mother of this son or daughter. However much they share, at the deepest level they suffer alone. In his book *The Anatomy of Loneliness* the writer Thomas Wolfe writes, 'The most tragic, sublime and beautiful expression of loneliness which I have ever read is the Book of Job.'[3] We need to recognize that those who suffer, suffer alone.

So let us go with Job into his dark lament. Perhaps the most prominent feature of this lament is that Job can only look back.

Job can only look back

Here is something that goes to the heart of human desperation. Desperation is the denial of hope. Hope looks forward; desperation can only relive the past and seek to rewrite it, or even to erase it. Human despair is fundamentally a turning away from the future and back to the past. We see this again and again in this lament.

In verses 3–10, Job curses his origins:

> Let the day perish on which I was born,
> and the night that said,
> 'A man is conceived.'
> (3:3) (NIV, 'A boy is *born*' is misleading here)

Job curses both the night of his conception and the day of his birth, the two critical points in his origins: 'Oh, that God would strike them out of the calendar forever!' He begins with his birthday (verses 4–5) and longs for that day to turn to *darkness*, so that (verse 5) *gloom and deep darkness* (the shadow of death) may reclaim it. In the beginning *darkness was over the face of the deep* (Genesis 1:2) and the Creator said, *Let there be light.* But Job says, 'I wish you would rewind the tape of Creation: let there be darkness.'

It is the same in verses 6–9 for the night of his conception. May it not just be a normal night, with starlight, but an utterly dark night (verse 6) – a spiritually dark night, like the plague of darkness over Egypt, or when John comments that Judas went out into the darkness, *And it was night* (John 13:30). 'Let it be a *barren* night (verse 7) with no new life, no sounds of delight such as accompanied my conception.' Verse 8 uses the language of ancient stories. *Leviathan* (whom we meet again in Job 41) was the sea-monster of chaos, the great enemy of the Creator whose purpose was to undo the order and beauty God had made. Job pictures Leviathan as having keepers, professional curse-bringers, who can whistle for Leviathan and call him to come and destroy part of the created order. 'I wish they would call him to curse the night of my conception, so that I might never have been,' he says. 'May that night go on forever (verse 9) with no dawn, no future, no hope.'

And why should that night be cursed? 'Because it allowed new life to come into my mother's womb' (verse 10), and 'it didn't *shut the doors.* And if it had *shut the doors* then all my troubles would not have been.' But Job has been conceived and born. So he continues in verses 11–19, 'If I had to be conceived and born, why did I stay alive? Why was I not stillborn? Why were there my mother's knees to hold me as I came from the womb, why were there breasts to suck? Why?' (verses 11–12).

'Because if I had not survived my birth, I would be at peace' (verse 13). 'I would have been in Sheol, the place of the dead. And that would be peace.' In his saner moments Job knows that is not true, that Sheol is a terrible place: in 17:14 he knows it is where the pit and the worm are your father and mother. But in his desperation he thinks it is the place (verse 17) where the wicked (like the Sabeans, 1:15, and Chaldeans, 1:17) cease from causing trouble for the righteous, and the weary can at last rest. And Job's pain goes beyond his own suffering. In verse 18 he is pained not only by his own suffering but by the unfair sufferings of others: at least in Sheol the prisoners are free from the harsh voice of the slave-driver.

It is a penetrating image, heavy with the long shadow of human cruelty over the lives of sufferers. At the very end of his classic and deeply moving two-volume account of Auschwitz and his return home, the Italian Jew Primo Levi recounts, 'a dream full of horror [which] has not ceased to visit me'. 'It is a dream within a dream' in which he begins in peace, perhaps sitting at table with family or friends, or in the green countryside. And yet he feels 'a deep and subtle anguish, the definite sensation of an impending threat'. And then

> everything collapses and disintegrates around me, the scenery, the walls, the people, while the anguish becomes more intense and more precise. Now everything has changed to chaos; I am alone in the centre of a grey and turbid nothing, and now, I *know* what this thing means, and I also know that I have always known it; I am in the Lager [concentration camp] once more, and nothing is true outside the Lager. All the rest was a brief pause, a decep-tion of the senses, a dream; my family, nature in flower, my home. Now this inner dream, this dream of peace, is over, and in the outer dream, which con-tinues, gelid, a well-known voice resounds: a single word, not imperious, but brief and subdued. It is the dawn command of Auschwitz, a foreign word, feared and expected: get up, '*Wstawàch*'.[4]

The voice of the slave-driver cast a long shadow, a nightmare shadow that never left him. Perhaps that voice echoed in his mind at the time of his death, possibly by suicide, in the 1960s.

Job is obsessed with death as the only way out of trouble, because life is so futile. Wilfred Owen gets this so poignantly in his poem 'Futility' (see page 28), as he moves from one futile tragedy to a whole world that seems to have no point. The sun used to wake this young man, but it will not wake him now. That same sun gave life to the cold earth (at creation): why not now to his cold earth? And in his anger he shouts, 'O what made fatuous sunbeams toil / To break earth's sleep at all?' Why did God bother to make the world at all? And so we are drawn by the tragedy of Job into bigger and more alarming questions. Job wants not only to undo his own life, but to question the Creation of the world. Genesis 1 moves from darkness to light, from night to day, from inanimacy to life. Job wants to put it all into reverse.

This is terrible. In normal life almost nothing can rival conception and birth as signs of hope. A wife tells us she is expecting a baby: we rejoice. Or we ought to. Her position is quite literally pregnant with hope (even if sometimes mixed with feelings of inconvenience, alarm or anxiety). But fundamentally there is excitement and there are eager preparations. And when we hear of a safe birth this is even more so. The whole affair is full of looking forward. We ask a couple of expectant parents, 'Is there anything you are looking forward to?', and they look at us as if we are mad. 'What a silly question! Of course we're looking forward. Our lives, and the mother's body, are literally filled with hope and expectation.'

But for Job it has all gone into the negative. All he sees is a 'No Entry' sign to the future. 'If only I had never been.'

'What are you looking forward to, Job?'

'Nothing.'

If he tries to look forward, all he can see is a blank wall of hopelessness, as his affections and longings are turned back upon themselves in despair. 'There is no future for me; and would that there had been no past.' Here is bitter memory unsweetened by hope.

In St Nicholas' church in the village of Moreton, Dorset, is a beautiful window engraved by Laurence Whistler. It is a memorial to a local fighter pilot shot down and killed in the Battle of Britain. It shows the broken propeller of his plane; and on it are two pairs of initials, his and his young wife's, with the years of their marriage: 1939–1940. What did that premature death do to that young widow? What happened in her mind to all the potential and hope with which their marriage began? The children they might have had, the future together. There is no comment in the window, but in those initials and those dates, such a compression of grief.

We know if we are Christians that for every believer the best is yet to be. Always better things are ahead; always there is hope because the future is God's future and our destiny is glory. But we need to recognize that there may be times in the life of a believer when that future appears utterly blank. And all we can do is look back with regret, consumed with 'if only'. That is where Job is in Job 3. It is a bleak time.

And yet even in his darkness, Job cannot avoid God.

Even in his darkness, Job cannot avoid God

It seems unlikely that Job is conscious of the presence of God. Perhaps Job would have echoed the words of C. S. Lewis in Lewis's moving personal reflection after the death of his wife (*A Grief Observed*). Lewis asks the question, in bereavement, 'Where is God?' and he answers:

> This is one of the most disquieting symptoms. When you are happy, so happy that you have no sense of needing Him, . . . if you remember yourself and turn to Him with gratitude and praise, you will be – or so it feels – welcomed with open arms.
>
> But go to him when your need is desperate, when all other help is vain, and what do you find? A door slammed in your face, and a sound of bolting and double bolting on the inside. After that, silence. You may as well turn away. The longer you wait, the more emphatic the silence will become. There are no lights in the windows. It might be an empty house. Was it ever inhabited? It seemed so once.[5]

And yet Job knows that he cannot turn away from that door. And right here in the depth of his misery he knows he has to deal with God. We shall see as the book unfolds that this is a great theme in his journey. Even in God's felt absence God is still somehow there. We see this in verse 23:

> *Why is light given to a man whose way is hidden,*
> *whom God has hedged in?*
> (3:23; see also 3:20)

In 1:10 Satan complained that God had put a protective hedge around Job. But now it is a hedge that hems him in, razor wire not to keep the marauder out, but to keep Job imprisoned in a miserable life he longs to leave, but cannot. And yet God has done it, and so he must deal with God. Even in his absence God is present as the focus of Job's loss. There is a glimmer of hope here. But it will take some time for that glimmer to become a ray. So at the end of Job 3 we leave Job terribly alone, sitting with friends who want to comfort him but have nothing to say. We leave him able only to look back with bitter regrets that he ever lived, mired in deep darkness. Is there anything that can be said to him?

I believe there is; even at this stage there is something to be said, beyond the silence of bankruptcy, beyond even the silence of sympathy. Because two thousand years ago another blameless believer was with three friends, in the garden of Gethsemane (Mark 14:32–42). And as he suffered in anticipation the agony of the cross, he too was deeply alone. *Could you not watch one hour?* (verse 38). But they could not. And then on the cross he too was in deep darkness. Deeper than the darkness of night. Deeper even than Job's darkness. And from his lips the cry of dereliction *My God, my God, why have you forsaken me?* (Mark 15:34).

And this believer has so plumbed the depths of human sorrow that he alone can walk with human beings in their sorrow. Someone has written:

> Suffering encloses a man in solitude . . . Between Job and his friends an abyss was cleft. They regarded him with astonishment as a strange being . . . But they could no longer get to him. Only Jesus could cross this abyss, descend into the abyss of misery, plunge into the deepest hell.[6]

And for this reason no sufferer now need ever be completely alone.

Notes

1. See Gaius Davies, *Genius, Grief and Grace* (Christian Focus, 2001), ch. 3.
2. Chris Williams, Paul Richards and Ingrid Whitton, *I'm Not Supposed to Feel Like This* (Hodder, 2002).
3. Quoted in *The Dimensions of Job: A Study and Selected Readings* ed. Nahum N. Glatzer (New York: Schocken Books, 1969), p. ix.
4. Primo Levi, *If This Is a Man* and *The Truce* (Penguin, 1979), pp. 379–380.
5. C. S. Lewis, *A Grief Observed* (Faber, 1966), p. 7.
6. Jean Danielou, quoted in *The Dimensions of Job: A Study and Selected Readings* ed. Nahum N. Glatzer (New York: Schocken Books, 1969), p. 109.

4 What not to say to the suffering believer (Job 4 – 27)

In the last chapter we considered the Christian hymnwriter William Cowper. In his hymn 'God moves in a mysterious way' Cowper assures us that 'Behind a frowning providence [God] hides a smiling face.' But is it true? When providence frowns and the believer's circumstances are filled with pain, is there a face smiling with sovereign love? Or is this a fancy, a sugary make-believe worthy only of the world of Walt Disney? Cowper himself, in times of deep depression, sometimes doubted the truth of his own hymn.

In Job 3 we heard Job utter a black, heart-rending lament of utter desolation. At the end we left him deeply alone and desperately devoid of hope, wanting the progress of the created order to be set into reverse, light to turn back to darkness and his life to dissolve in death. It was a bleak chapter. The chapter ended with a terrible question ringing in our ears. This blameless believer whose possessions are all lost, his children killed and his health destroyed, cries out, *Why?* (3:20, 23). Why indeed? We must ask this question. For, as has been said, it is not suffering that destroys a man, but suffering without a purpose. Why? What do we say, to ourselves when we sit where Job sat, or to others when we sit with them, as Job's three friends did?

There is a time for saying nothing. A time when trauma so numbs feeling that words lose their usefulness, when loss cauterizes the senses and all someone can do is stare blankly into space, and all we can do is sit alongside and maybe hold a hand. But after that the question comes: Why?

So what do we say? And not just afterwards. What do we say before suffering comes? At an Anglican ordination the ordinand is charged 'to prepare the dying for their death'. Although the intention here may be the narrower one of ministry to those near the point of death, the charge has wider implications. For all Christians ought to be engaged in preparing one another for their deaths, and for suffering. So that when suffering comes we may be so shaped by God's Word that we may be able, as it were, to put our hands into the hand of God even in the darkness.

The Lutheran pastor Helmut Thielicke, preaching in Stuttgart near the end of the second world war, during the period of heavy allied bombing, tells this story. He was walking discouraged through the city, absorbed in gloomy thoughts, when he found himself looking down into the concrete pit of a cellar that had been shattered by a bomb, and in which more than fifty young people had been killed:

> A woman came up to me and asked whether I was [Pastor Thielicke], since she was not sure who I was in the clothes I wore. Then she said, 'My husband died down there. His place was right under the hole. The clean-up squad was unable to find a trace of him; all that was left was his cap. We were there the last time you preached in the cathedral church. And here before this pit I want to thank you for preparing him for eternity.'[1]

The privilege of speaking with sufferers is one that is easily abused. In this chapter we are going to learn from the mistakes of three men who said a great deal to a sufferer, although it was not very helpful: Eliphaz, Bildad and Zophar, Job's Comforters, as they are ironically called. They say nothing for a week (2:11ff.). But after Job's lament (chapter 3) they say much. They speak nine Bible chapters in nearly three rounds of heated argument. In this chapter we look at what they say to Job, and in the next two chapters we consider some of Job's answers. In order to let the book of Job have its way with us, we ought properly to let each speech and each answer

from Job sink slowly into our hearts and minds. But in a brief introductory study we have to speed up. On our journey, we have, as it
were, trekked quietly on foot through Job 1 – 3. Now we must do an
aerial survey of the next section of terrain.

The three friends are not clones of each other in what they say,
and there is also a measure of development in their speeches as we
move through the three cycles. But by and large they say the same
things in similar ways, and for the purposes of this section we consider them together so that we are introduced to the common salient
features of their woeful pastoral theology.

Before reading this chapter, it would be helpful to read some examples of the friends' speeches, to get the flavour. For example, we
might read the words of Eliphaz in Job 15. In Job 12 – 14 Job says, 'I
can't understand why this is happening to me. I haven't done anything especially wrong to deserve this.' Read Job 15 to see how and
why Eliphaz is not impressed by Job's protestations.

Now read Job 21 and 22. In Job 21 Job makes the point that if you
look around the world you will notice that people who do not care
about God live long happy lives and die peacefully in their sleep. Read
Job 22 to see what Eliphaz makes of that.

Here are three preliminary points to help us get the feel of these
exchanges.

The comforters are not impressed with Job

For example, in 8:2 Bildad is clearly riled by Job: 'Your words are a
blustering wind! Why don't you shut up, you old windbag? You are
talking a lot of hot air.' Eliphaz says much the same in 15:2–3. For
while Job's appearance had made his friends sad (2:12), his words
make them angry. Why? Because, as the exchanges go on, repeatedly
Job insists he is not being punished for some particular sin, for he has
nothing on his conscience that can justify this treatment from God.
So it seems that God is being unfair. This makes his friends livid. We
can understand why.

So in 11:2–6 Zophar wishes that God will intervene and speak,
because that will shut Job up and show him what empty babble he is
pouring out. (It never crosses Zophar's mind that God might actually
do this, let alone what God's verdict might be on him and his friends,

42:7.) As the exchanges continue, Job's friends become thoroughly fed up with having to listen to him (e.g. 18:2a). They wish he will shut up and listen properly to them.

Job is not impressed with his comforters

If the friends are unimpressed with Job, Job is not exactly filled with gratitude towards them. The antipathy and frustration are mutual. There is, in diplomatic language, 'a full and frank exchange of views'. Job had hoped for refreshment from them, but they were like a river bed to which a parched traveller turns aside, only to find it dry as dust (6:14–30). 'Miserable comforters are you all!' (16:2, and again in verse 3 he calls them windbags and wishes they would shut up). Or hear the biting sarcasm of Job in 12:2: 'Oh, yes, you are so wise! You are where wisdom is. When you die, I am really worried that there won't be any wise people left in the world.' This is sharp and cutting sarcasm (cf. 26:2–3). It is prompted by the error and cruelty of his friends. For they torment Job and break him in pieces with their words (19:2).

For twenty-four chapters (Job 4 – 27) Job and his friends have a blazing row. So who is right to be angry? Are the friends right to be angry because Job accuses God of being unfair? Or is Job right to be angry with the friends for not offering him any substantial comfort? It would be helpful to know, and we are told at the end of the book. For at the end the Lord says to Eliphaz, *My anger burns against you and against your two friends, for you have not spoken of me what is right . . .* (42:7)

And so we learn that God is not impressed with Job's comforters.

God is not impressed with Job's comforters

The anger of Job at his friends is an echo of the anger of God that burns against them.

So we are looking in this chapter at nine Bible chapters that are, by and large, a load of rubbish. Except, in a way, they are not. Because much of what they say would probably have us putting ticks in the margin. If it were total rubbish that would be much easier. It is always like that with false teaching; dangerous because it is nearly true. So we shall need to look carefully at where Job's comforters go wrong.

We consider in turn their system of theology, their pastoral tone and their gaps or omissions (the vital things they do not believe).

Their system

The system of theology that underlies all three friends is simple and clear.

- God is absolutely in control. (We have seen that this is indeed one of the foundational markers laid down by our narrator in Job 1 and 2.)
- God is absolutely just and fair.
- *Therefore* he always punishes wickedness and blesses righteousness, always (and pretty soon and certainly in this life). For if he were ever to do otherwise he must necessarily be unjust, which is inconceivable.
- *Therefore*, if I suffer, I *must* have sinned and am being punished justly for my sin. (And, presumably, if I am blessed, I must have been good – although this isn't relevant here, so they do not develop this side of it.)

This logic undergirds almost all they say. For example, 'Consider now: Who, being innocent, ever perished?' (4:7). 'You see', implies Eliphaz, 'if the innocent did perish, the world would be unfair, and that cannot be.' Again, in 5:17–26 Eliphaz says, 'Job, your suffering is God's discipline. You sinned, and because God loves you he disciplines you. So learn from his discipline.' Now the Bible does teach the truth that God disciplines his spiritual child, in Proverbs 3:11–12 (quoted in Hebrews 12:4–13). It is an entirely valid argument, *assuming* that Job has sinned. And Eliphaz 'knows' Job has sinned, because he sees Job suffering.

The emotional stakes are raised in 8:4–7, where Bildad draws another conclusion from their system. 'So, your children died, did they, Job? Well, that means they must have sinned.' This is of questionable comfort to Job, even though Bildad interprets their way of thinking sensitively and tells Job (verses 5–7) that it may not be too late for Job himself. 'If you repent, God may yet restore you.' Again, within the terms of their mindset, this is all correct.

The friends' frustration with Job is becoming evident where Zophar pushes things even further: *Know then that God exacts of you less than your guilt deserves* (11:6b). 'God has even forgotten or overlooked some of your sin, Job. (For presumably if he hadn't, you'd already be dead like your children.)' Zophar is fed up with Job's protestations of innocence. 'Think yourself lucky God hasn't really punished you for all your sins!' And then again, as with Bildad in 8:4–7, in verses 13–19 there is another appeal for Job to repent as they deduce that he ought.

The reason the friends feel so strongly about it all is that they have grasped that unless God is just and fair, the moral fabric of the universe will disintegrate. We see this in the imagery of 18:3–5, where Bildad complains (verse 3) that Job is treating them as stupid. Job is getting very angry (4a), but it is outrageous of him to imagine (4b) that *the earth* may be *forsaken for you, or the rock be removed out of its place*; that is, that the moral order and structure of the cosmos can be rearranged just to suit one individual's whims. 'You cannot expect a cosmic exception to be made for you, Job. No (verse 5), it is an absolute rule that *the light of the wicked is put out . . .* So, if you are suffering, you must be wicked.' And so it goes on. But Job won't accept it. He stubbornly refuses to repent of sins he hasn't committed. His conscience is clear.

And so in 22:5–9 Eliphaz loses his rag and tells Job precisely what he has done wrong:

Is not your evil abundant?
   There is no end to your iniquities.
(22:5)

'And I'll be specific, Job, since you force me to it. You're a rich man, aren't you? Well, don't expect us to believe you got rich quite as honestly and justly and kindly as you would have us think! Admit it: come clean, you hypocrite!' And again (22:21–30) there is an appeal for Job to repent. It is a winsome appeal, and a very beautiful expression of the offer of the gospel. I remember a Bible study at a Christian youth camp on this very passage. But it was wrenched out of its context, which is of utterly inappropriate words directed to the wrong man.

So here is the comforters' outlook. Both sides of this system lie deep in the human psyche. We see one side of the formula in the musical *The Sound of Music*. The handsome Count declares his love for the young heroine. And in her delight she sings her sweet but deeply untrue deduction that . . . somewhere in my youth or child-hood, I must have done something good. Something good has happened to me, and therefore I deduce that in order to deserve this, 'I must have done something good.' The comforters would agree.

The other side of the comforters' world-view surfaced when an elderly Christian lady said to me, as she suffered much pain in old age, 'Have I done something terribly wrong? What have I *done* to deserve this?' And when a dear Christian friend of mine, suffering deep depression, cried out, 'I must have done something terrible in the past,' the comforters say, 'Yes, you must.'

What are we to make of this theological system? It will not do to dismiss it out of hand as stupid. For it is not stupid. The first two parts of their formula (page 41) are right. God is absolutely in control and God is absolutely just and fair. Further, we need to rec-ognize that there are many ways in which we may and do suffer as a direct result of our own sin. In Psalm 32 the psalmist says that when he kept his sin secret, the pressure of unresolved guilt was destroy-ing him physically. And only when he confessed it and turned from it, did his health return. If I get drunk and drive and crash and injure myself, it is my fault. If I commit adultery and it leads, as it typically does, to misery and often violence (Proverbs 6:32–35) then that misery is the result of my sin. If someone hurts me and I will not forgive them, and I nurse resentment and become a hard and bitter person, then the damage to my character is my fault, because I ought to forgive.

So the comforters might be right when they appeal to Job to repent. And yet we remember that three times in Job 1 – 2 (once from the narrator, 1:1, and twice from the Lord, 1:8; 2:3) we have been told that Job is blameless. So the comforters make a big mistake. Job does not need to repent for any sin that has led to his suffering. He is not being punished for sin. To say that he is, adds a cruel burden to his grief. The comforters say it for nine chapters.

So let us jettison their way of thinking.

Their tone

They are very sure they are right. For example, at the end of Eliphaz's first speech he says, *'this we have searched out; it is true* [5:27]. So you'd better listen, Job.' The reason they are sure is that their authority is that of tradition (8:8–10). 'This was the tradition handed down to us,' they say, 'so it must be true'. (They forget the saying of Cyprian, that a tradition may just be an error in its old age.)

Again, in 15:7–10 Eliphaz pulls rank on Job: *What do you know that we do not know?* (verse 9). 'We are senior to you, more experienced' (verse 10). For the friends there is no puzzle or enigma in the world as they observe it. There is no chink in their dogmatic armour. It is all so tidy, so well swept. Whatever we do, we must not let evidence get in the way of a good theory.

Why are they so confident?

1. *They have no honesty.* They have inherited these dogmas, and they are not prepared actually to look at the world as it is. But they ought to. Because God's truth fits with God's world. When we look at the world through the spectacles of God's Word the world comes into focus and makes sense. We do not take our theory and squeeze the world into its mould. There is an air of unreality about their theology; it just does not fit the real world. It may work in the ghetto when everyone agrees to believe it and does not look too closely outside; but it has no power and no persuasiveness for those outside.

2. *They have no sympathy.* They do not seem to have been where Job is. So in 4:2–5 Eliphaz says, in effect, 'I can't quite see why you should be so miserable, Job. You used to be the one offering comfort to others, and I must admit you were very good at it. Well, that wasn't so difficult when you weren't suffering; but now it's your turn and you don't like it, do you?' They are sorry for him, at the start. But they don't understand his pain. They are more attached to their theories than to Job their friend. It is a little like the quip attributed to the author James Dobson, who said about parenting: 'I used to have 4 theories on child-rearing and no kids. Now I have 4 kids and no theories.' These comforters have plenty of theories about suffering, but we wonder if they have ever been there.

3. *They have no love.* It does not look as if the friends really love Job, for they do not listen to his cries. The cycles of speeches are like dialogues in which one side (the friends) are deaf to the cries and protestations of the other. They do not respond to what he says and engage with him as a fellow human being in need. The German writer Goethe once said that we can only understand what we love. This is true in all human relationships. Because they do not love Job, they cannot understand him.

And so we should avoid their tone even as we jettison their system.

What they don't believe

The trouble with the comforters is that so much of what they say looks right. It would be a useful exercise to read their speeches with a pencil in hand, and to put a tick in the margin against every statement they make with which we agree. There would be many ticks, and generally high marks for doctrinal orthodoxy. So much so that it is easy to think the friends are doctrinally sound teachers whose fault is simply that they are pastorally insensitive. But more careful consideration suggests that their fault lies deeper than pastoral insensitivity. It is the content, and not only the tone, of their teaching that is false. Their problem is not so much what they say as what they leave unsaid. (This is so often the case with false teaching; we need to be on the lookout not only for wrong teaching Bible teachers give, but also for vital biblical ingredients they habitually omit.)

There are three vital truths they don't believe.

No Satan

They have no place in their thinking for Satan. We know from Job 1 and 2 that Satan is a real and influential spiritual person. We know that the whole tragedy of Job has its origin in heavenly arguments between the Lord and Satan. But the comforters have no place in their thinking for Satan or for the spiritual battle. There are hints that Job does believe in Satan, however, in Job 3:8 where he speaks of Leviathan, and in Job 26:12–13 where he refers to Rahab the serpent monster (another expression in Old Testament symbolism of the great spiritual enemy of the Creator God); we shall return to Leviathan when we reach Job 41. But the friends have no place for spiritual forces of evil. In their world evil is purely a human phenomenon. It has no spiritual dimension; there is no spiritual battle. How wrong they are.

No waiting

For them, judgment is now. The wicked are punished now; the righteous are blessed now. But the promises of judgment are not for now. They are for the end. So, for example, Psalm 1 has a clear distinction between the righteous and the wicked. But it is *in the judgment* (verse 5) that the wicked will not stand. And the judgment is (usually) not yet. The comforters' 'now' theology seems so neat; but is actually disastrous. It is like a slot machine: put in some goodness and out pops a can of blessing. Put in some badness and out pops a can of poison. Just like that. In terms of the popular *Matrix* trilogy of films, they would think of a god like a deterministic computer program, a part of how the Matrix is operating, with fixed rules that determine how it all runs.

There is a *Peanuts* cartoon in which Lucy says to Charlie Brown, 'There is one thing you're going to have to learn: you reap what you sow, you get out of life what you put into it, no more and no less.' And Snoopy the dog mutters from the corner, 'I'd kind of like to see a little margin for error.' The Bible does indeed teach that we will reap what we sow (Galatians 6:7ff.); in the end there will be no 'margin for error'. But not immediately, because what we sow has to grow until harvest. In Jesus' parable (Matthew 13:24–30) the wheat and the weeds grow together. And they will not be separated until harvest (the last judgment). Then the wicked will be punished and the righteous saved, but not until then. The comforters are right to believe in retributive justice; they are wrong to assume that it will necessarily be immediate retributive justice. There will one day be a world ordered as it was at the creation, but we are not there yet.

But what are we to make of Bible passages that seem to speak quite straightforwardly of blessings following obedience and curses following apostasy? For example:

let your heart keep my commandments,
for length of days and years of life and peace they will add to you.
(Proverbs 3:1–2)

And yet they brought no peace to Job! (Many other examples could be taken, especially from Proverbs and Deuteronomy.)

There is a distinction between the general truth of such sayings and absolute 'every case' truth. There is perhaps an analogy with an ordered city after an earthquake. Suppose an earthquake struck a well-planned city, such as the Georgian 'New Town' of Edinburgh with its clear planning and gracious order. If I wanted to go from A to B afterwards, I would in general still be best advised to go by the main roads. But whereas before the earthquake that would always be the best route, now I might find both that the main road was blocked and also that some building had collapsed to open up some unplanned route. It is a little like this with the created order after the disruption of the fall of humankind. In general to keep God's commandments, to live in line with created order, will bring peace and prosperity; in general, for example, if I am honest and work hard I will do better. But not always. And the final proof that righteousness pays will not come until the final judgment, when the disruption will be put right and the creation reordered as it ought to be.

But the comforters turn religion into an impersonal slot-machine formula. There is no hoping for a future promised, but only living in the present. There is no prayer to a God unseen, but only moralizing. There is no love for a hidden God, or love for people in pain, but only well-swept answers. There is no personal yearning and longing and faith, but only sight. And so faith, hope and love are dissolved into moralism and lectures. There is a kind of Christianity that belongs to this family, that revels in the immediate. I expect the blessing of God now; I expect to see the triumph of God now; I expect to know the answers now. There is to be no waiting. We shall see in the next chapter how very different it is with Job himself.

No cross

In the context of the whole Bible, perhaps the deepest error and omission of the friends is this: they have no place for innocent suffering. They think that if the righteous were ever to suffer or perish it would be a blot on the moral landscape. As Eliphaz asks, *who that was innocent ever perished?* (4:7).

The Bible places against that question a large eternal cross.

The innocent One perished in the place of the guilty, so that we might not finally perish. In a profound sense, the sufferings of Job are the price to unlock grace. Or, to be more accurate, the sufferings that Job foreshadows will be the price paid by grace to unlock the gate of heaven. With their tidy impersonal theological code, the comforters miss the heart of the universe.

Notes

1. Helmut Thielicke, *The Prayer that Spans the World: Sermons on the Lord's Prayer* (English translation James Clarke, 1960), pp. 65–67.

5 Two marks of a real believer (Job 4 – 27)

An impressive sports car pulled up and parked just in front of my family. We waited with some interest to see what powerful and impressive human being would get out. For surely with such a fine car on the outside, the driver inside must be equally awesome. To our dismay a pot-bellied balding unshaven scruff of a man emerged and waddled away. This is a parable. For the exterior may mask a very different reality inside. In this chapter we are going to watch as the opposite happens, as a deeply unimpressive exterior is peeled back to reveal an interior of infinite value. We are going to watch as a true worshipper of God is revealed. We are going to see two marks of the real believer. Both marks are deeply paradoxical. They cut right across all human instincts about religion. These hallmarks of a true worshipper are utterly contradictory to what we might expect.

In the last chapter we surveyed Job's 'Comforters', his three friends who so signally failed to offer him any substantial comfort. We noted in particular the three glaring omissions in their thinking about God that ruin their tidy theological system: no Satan, no waiting and no cross. In this chapter and the next we focus on Job's replies, from his eight speeches in Job 4 – 27. In this chapter we look at Job himself, while in the next we focus on Job 19 and consider the God of Job.

Sometimes in the council chamber of heaven, God looks down at the earth, points and says to Satan, 'Look at Simon there: he's a real believer.' Or 'Look at Nicola there: she really worships me.' We may be sure that Satan replies, as he did for Job, 'Oh, you think so, do you, Lord? Well, I admit they do look a bit like believers on the outside. But I doubt very much if you'll find a real worshipper inside.' And God says, 'It's very important for us to know publicly without doubt whether he or she is a real worshipper. So you take away from her the externals, what she values – and then we'll see. Take away from her some precious relationship, frustrate some hope, inflict some pain, and then we'll all publicly see if she is a real worshipper. Face him with serious loss, strip away his security, dent his status, and then the real person will step out and we'll see.'

That is the conversation of Job 1 – 2. What is the only sure test by which the world will know who are real worshippers of the true God and who are just pretending? Answer: loss and suffering. The only sure test is to strip from worshippers something of value, and then we shall see if they really worship the living God and bow down to him simply because he is God. Only when worship comes at a cost may we tell if it is true. Suffering is the fire that refines and reveals the heart of worship. We see this again and again in church life when it costs to follow Christ. A Christian wants to marry a non-Christian, knowing it will be a union in which at the deepest level they will pull in opposite directions. It will cost to break the relationship off and worship God wholeheartedly. That is when true worship is revealed. It costs to be an open Christian at school or college or in the office. Perhaps a loss of face, a loss of prestige or reputation. It is loss that reveals the true worshipper and separates the fair-weather Christian from the true worshipper.

We are going to watch in this section a true worshipper revealed. And we may be surprised by the hallmarks that mark him out as the real thing. For on the outside Job is alone, scratching at his agonized skin, sitting on the rubbish dump outside the city gate (2:8). He has no status, no job, no family and no hope. And yet we shall see here, despised and rejected, outside the city wall, the pure gold of a real believer. In Shakespeare's words:

Sweet are the uses of adversity,

Which, like the toad, ugly and venomous,

Wears yet a precious jewel in his head.[1]

We are going to see the precious jewel of real worship in the midst of ugliness and venom. And as we see this precious jewel unveiled, we remember a later believer hanging naked outside the city wall, despised, rejected – and yet precious beyond compare.

So as we look at Job's side of the cycles of speeches we shift our focus from these three comforters, so confident, so impressive – and so wrong. And we listen to Job in his laments, so pathetic, so poignant, so confused, so full of doubt – and so deeply right with God. These are rich chapters that repay slow, thoughtful reading, so their riches and puzzles soak into us. But again, as in the last chapter, we must be content with an aerial tour.

Here are two hallmarks of a real worshipper, revealed by suffering.

A unique pain

There is a pain for the believer that gives suffering a unique sharpness. Suffering is the common experience of the human race. All sorts of people get ill; all kinds of people are touched by war, famine and earthquake. And yet suffering touches the believer with a sharper and uniquely piercing pain. How so? Believers do not necessarily and always suffer more or worse. They do not get more illnesses or suffer worse from natural disasters. So in what way is the pain of a believer sharper?

It is what is sometimes called the problem of pain. The worshipper truly believes that God is sovereign. He or she really believes that the living God is in control of his world. And so, when suffering comes, it must be God who sends it – after all, he is in control, is he not? It is not just that it hurts – although Job's suffering hurts abominably. It is more than this: it is the conviction that it is God who is doing the hurting. We see this in Job's first reply (Job 6 – 7). In Job 6:2–4 Job laments that God is like an archer firing poison arrows at him. He returns to this image in Job 7:17–21, where in a parody of Psalm 8 he asks, *What is man, that you make so much of him . . . ?*

Where Psalm 8 marvels at the dignity entrusted to human beings, of caring for God's world, Job cannot see it. For him, God simply will not leave him alone, but insists on choosing Job to be his target for archery target practice (verse 20). God is an accuser who picks legalistically over his past (verse 21a), a God with no grace and no forgiveness. And it's so unfair. 'Because', he says in effect, 'I have confessed my sin, I am a real believer, I am living a new life. So why, oh why, does God persist in finding fault with me?' (cf. 13:26). I do not deserve it. We find similar complaints in the psalms (e.g. Psalm 44).

And it is not just Job. For the injustice Job experiences is targeted at others as well. In 9:21–24 he says he is past caring about himself. But this kind of thing is happening all over the place. So much so that he casts in God's face a terrible accusation: *He destroys both the blameless and the wicked* (verse 22). That is a very serious accusation; no wonder Job's friends see red. For if that kind of accusation can be proved against a judge or government minister then he or she must resign, if there is to be any justice. 'I really think', implies Job, 'that God ought to resign. But it's a true accusation,' says Job, 'for when an epidemic brings sudden death; God mocks the despair of the innocent (verse 23). When a land falls into the hands of the wicked, *he* blindfolds its judges – so that there is no justice. *If it is not he, who then is it?*' (verse 24). That last is a deeper question than Job maybe realized, as we who have read Job 1 and 2 know. Whose hand is doing this? This is a question to which we shall return.

In 16:7–14 Job experiences God as some kind of 'cosmic sadist' (in C. S. Lewis's memorable phrase). (We shall see when we come to the monster Leviathan, in Job 41, that what Job perceives as 'God' attacking him is not quite so simple.) It all seems to Job to be deeply unfair. And yet surely God is just, isn't he? This is the added pain for the believer of living in a world of undeserved suffering. For undeserved suffering is a threat to the moral foundations of the universe. Either God is not in control or he is not fair. And that causes the believer deep and sharp perplexity.

We saw in the last chapter how Job's comforters get around this problem by dogmatic denial. Undeserved suffering never happens. How do we know? Well, if someone suffers it proves they deserve it. This is a circular argument, clung to at the price of honesty. Their world-view can be believed only if we close our eyes to the reality of the world we are supposed to be viewing, where there are believers with a clear conscience, with no hidden sin, trusting in God for forgiveness and walking in the light with him, and yet who yet suffer terribly.

It is a problem. But it is important for us to notice that it is a problem only for the believer. When unbelievers say to us they are troubled by the problem of pain and the unfairness of suffering in the world, we may say to them, 'Why are *you* troubled? *I* as a believer am troubled, but why should you be? For you do not believe in a living God who is in control and who is good. So why should you expect there to be any logic or any fairness? And yet you do, don't you? I wonder if that is because we are deeply hard-wired to know there is a living God who is in control and who is just.' The irony is that the moment we begin to feel this perplexity we must admit we ought to believe in a living God.

And if you and I don't feel this pain, it must be questioned whether we really believe. A survivor of Auschwitz once wrote:

> It never occurred to me to question God's doings or lack of doings while I was an inmate of Auschwitz . . . I was no less or no more religious because of what the Nazis did to us; and I believe my faith in God was not undermined in the least. It never occurred to me to associate the calamity we were experiencing with God, to blame Him . . . because He didn't come to our aid.[2]

That sounds a fine example of resilient faith; but it is actually the mark of an unbeliever. For the believer will follow Job and rail passionately against the injustice of it all, calling on the sovereign God to do something. The believer takes seriously the 'godness' of God.

The Christian poet Gerard Manley Hopkins understood this, in this poem, inspired by Jeremiah's complaint in Jeremiah 12:1ff.:

> THOU art indeed just, Lord, if I contend
> With thee; but, sir, so what I plead is just.
> Why do sinners' ways prosper? and why must
> Disappointment all I endeavour end?
>
> Wert thou my enemy, O thou my friend,
> How wouldst thou worse, I wonder, than thou dost

Defeat, thwart me? Oh, the sots and thralls of lust
Do in spare hours more thrive than I that spend,
Sir, life upon thy cause. See, banks and brakes
Now leavèd how thick! lacèd they are again
With fretty chervil, look, and fresh wind shakes
Them; birds build – but not I build; no, but strain,
Time's eunuch, and not breed one work that wakes.
Mine, O thou lord of life, send my roots rain.

The first mark of a real believer is to feel keenly the pain of an unfair world. The unbeliever says to us, 'Have you ever wondered why the world is so unfair?'

'Oh, yes,' we say. 'We wonder all the time.'

A passionate longing

The second mark of the believer is equally paradoxical: although Job accuses God of being unfair, he longs and yearns with all his being to bring his case to God. We saw in Job 1 and 2 a heavenly council or courtroom in which matters of justice in the universe were sorted out. A kind of supreme High Court presided over by the Creator, the Lord Chief Justice. And Job says, 'I want leave to appeal to this court.' His comforters say, 'Don't be stupid: *Call now; is there anyone who will answer you?*' (5:1) (We shall see the answer from Job 38 onwards). But, although scared stiff, Job insists on calling.

The tension between his terror and his longing is vivid in Job 9:3:

If one wished to contend with him [God],
  one could not answer him once in a thousand times.

And so he goes on. 'I'm the little man,' he says. It is somewhat like a courtroom drama where the feisty underdog stands up bravely to the powerful corporate lawyers, as Julia Roberts does in *Erin Brockovich*. 'It's just little me against the God who made the world,' says Job. 'I haven't a chance. I know I'm innocent, but I haven't a chance' (verse 15). It is so unfair.

And in verses 32–35 he laments the fact that there is no arbiter or mediator to see fair play between him and God (or possibly expresses his longing that there might be such a one).

Although Job is terrified, he longs to speak to God face to face. This is the mark of a true worshipper. Even when I cannot understand what God is doing, I know it is God with whom I have to deal – because he is God. That is what it is to be a worshipper: to bow down before the one who alone is God.

But it is easy and understandable to give up. When the famous Bible translator J. B. Phillips was 5 his mother got cancer. She suffered terribly for ten years and died when he was 15. All through his childhood he watched her waste away. He said of that time, 'I gave up my religious faith utterly, for what use was prayer and talk of the love of God when I returned daily to this horrible caricature of the sprightly, witty mother I had known and loved.'[3]

It was only later he came back to Christ. We can understand that.

And yet even in the depths of his suffering Job cannot give up. Again and again, because he loves God, he says, 'I want to meet God. I want to be right with God. I want to be reconciled to God. I want to be justified, vindicated, seen to be right with God.' *Though he slay me, I will hope in him* (13:15). He must set his hope in God, for there is nowhere else he can turn. He is like the psalmist in Psalm 84:5, *in whose heart are the highways to Zion.*

He longs above all the longings of the human heart to be in the presence of God. We see this longing in 14:13–17, where he yearns for restoration of fellowship with God. He knows that to be a human being is to be made for the love of God. He cannot bear to think himself cast away (23:3).

The point is this. Job says some hard things against God. He almost says he hates him. And yet it is rather like those scenes in a love drama. There is a troubled relationship and the girl shouts at her lover, 'I hate you. Why do you do this to me? I hate you.' And yet we know she loves him. And she longs for him to prove to her that he is not the hateful man she perceives him to be. She longs for him to love her. Job shouts at God in that spirit, 'Why, why, why are you doing this to me?' Desperately he longs to meet his terrifying, mysterious God, the God he does not understand and yet the God he needs and the God he loves. This is true worship, revealed by suffering.

If we are Christian people, we ought to be deeply challenged by this mark of the believer. Do we in our church fellowships long passionately for God? Do we as individual Christians long urgently and desperately for God? If we do, we shall pray. The comforters would not have bothered to come to their church prayer meeting. After all, they would have reasoned, it is all being sorted out automatically by God anyway. But Job would have been there every time.

Jesus taught this in Luke 18:1–8, using the image of the widow in an unfair world, desperate for justice, pestering the unjust judge until he gives way. 'How much more', says Jesus, 'ought the believer to pray to the judge of all the earth and not give up!' And yet he concludes, *Nevertheless, when the Son of Man comes, will he find faith on earth?* (verse 8). If the Lord Jesus returns tomorrow, will he find in us that deep longing for God that pours itself out in prayer? Will he find our church meetings for prayer overflowing – overflowing with people so that we could not fit into our buildings, and overflowing with prayer? Or will he find a bunch of lukewarm orthodox respectables going through the motions? Are we true worshippers? Neither knowledge, nor experience, nor music, nor what happens in our meetings will reveal the answer. But suffering and loss will.

Notes

1. *As you Like it*, Act II, Scene 1.
2. Quoted in Harold Kushner, *When Bad Things Happen to Good People* (HarperCollins, 1981), pp. 85–86.
3. Quoted in Gaius Davies, *Genius, Grief and Grace* (Christian Focus, 2001), pp. 313–314.

6 Is God for me or against me? (Job 19)

We saw in the last chapter two paradoxical marks of a true worshipper: a unique pain, of seeing a world that ought to be well ordered gone terribly wrong; and yet a passionate longing for the God who is – or ought to be – running this troubled world. These two marks together, paradoxical as they are, issue in a life deeply marked by pain and by prayer. At the heart of the pain is the tension between the 'god' who seems to be running this world and the God we hope and trust is actually doing so. For the character of the one seems so puzzlingly at odds with the perfection of the other.

In a way, the deepest question Job faces is this: 'Is God for me or against me?' For ultimately nothing else matters. If God be for me, on my side, then ultimately nothing and no-one can do me lasting harm and I shall emerge as more than a conqueror (Psalm 56:9; Romans 8:31–39). But if God is against me, then my despair is well grounded in objective reality.

This question lies beneath the question 'Why?' that echoes through the book of Job (from 3:20, 23 onwards) and on through the history of believers in pain. It is such a common question, but such a real one. 'Why did she die?' asks a widower. 'We had such plans for our retirement, and now – nothing, and I am so alone.'

'Why did he get Alzheimer's?' asks the elderly wife. 'So that from now on it's just an agonizing, weary oh-so-gradual bereavement. Why did that have to happen? As I watch him whom I love fade away into absurdity and confusion.'

'Why did I get into this job,' asks another troubled Christian, 'which is working out so badly, so full of frustration?'

'Why was my childhood so difficult?' asks another. 'Why did my parents split, leaving such a long shadow of pain and insecurity in me? Why did that have to happen, so that I live with the consequences every day?'

'Why was my son born handicapped,' asks a weary mother, 'so that all those childhood years were shot through with exhaustion and the bittersweet pain of caring for one who will never fulfil the potential of other babies? Why?'

Or, to put all these questions another way, 'What was going on in heaven to make this happen? Whose purpose was it, if there is a purpose? By whose doing, by whose agency, did this thing happen? Whose hand did this?' Or, to put it most sharply, 'Is God for me or against me? What kind of God is it who does what he did to Job, who traps a believer in a prison of barbed wire in suffering, loneliness, pain and misery?' 'You see,' says the Christian, 'I read in the Bible that God loves me, that he cares about me, that he is for me. But if I'm honest it doesn't seem like that. There are times when it feels like God is against me. So perhaps he is?'

Of all Job's laments, Job 19 focuses most sharply on this crucial question. It leads us to the heart of the book. The problem with the question 'Is God for me or against me?' is that we all know the Sunday school answer. We know the answer we are meant to give. Of course God is for us if we are in Christ (Romans 8:31–39). It is the answer we long to give. And yet – Job is too honest just to let that pat answer trip off his tongue, or to be fobbed off with the answer he is meant to give. 'No,' he says. 'I can't say that without being totally unreal.' The first part of his speech in Job 19 makes this clear.

The monster god (19:1–22)

The monster god has attacked me unfairly (19:1–12)

Verses 1–22 centre on what we may call 'the monster god'. Job experiences a god who is deeply, irrationally and unfairly hostile towards him. He vividly describes this monstrous spiritual being from verse 6 onwards. But first he reproaches his friends for not supporting him. 'It is enough to have God against me,' he says. 'Why must you too *torment me / and break me in pieces with words?*' (verse 2). For that is just what they have been doing. In Job 18 Bildad gives a blood-curdling description of all the terrors that await the wicked; and the clear implication is that this wicked man is precisely Job. 'You suffer, Job? You feel that God is against you? Dead right he is. Because you're a sinner and it's time you repented.' That is their message. And Job protests:

> And even if it be true that I have erred,
>   my error remains with myself.
> (19:4)

This seems to mean that it is between Job and God, and God knows he has nothing on his conscience.

In verses 6–12 Job goes on to say that it is bad enough that God is against him, without the added misery of his friends turning against him too. For here in verses 6–12 is a god who is deeply hostile to Job. He counts Job as a guilty man (verse 6), and therefore *closed his net* [the hunter's trap] *about me.* Job says it is unfair, *Behold, I cry out, 'Violence!'* (verse 7), implicitly appealing for someone to come to his aid against an armed robber or mugger, *but I am not answered; / I call for help, but there is no justice.* Quite the reverse. For (verse 8) the God who ought to give me justice *has walled up my way, so that I cannot pass, / and he has set darkness upon my paths.* He strips from Job his *glory* (verse 9), his reputation for integrity, drives him to breakdown and removes from him all hope (9–10). Why? *He has kindled his wrath against me / and counts me as his adversary* (verse 11).

The root problem is that Job is not justified or vindicated or accounted as righteous in the sight of God, but is rather counted as guilty and is therefore the object of wrath. The root issue is justification; Job longs to be accounted as righteous and publicly vindicated. But he is treated as guilty. And God is like some kind of vicious monster who tears at him with his claws, uproots his hope, with his vicious anger (11) burning against him, like some kind of fire-breathing dragon.

Verse 12 is extremely pathetic. Here are all the armies of the Lord of hosts advancing in force, preparing to lay siege. And to what great city are they laying siege? 'Just little me, little old Job in my one-man tent!' It is as if one of us goes for a night's camping on our own. We wake, peep out of the tent and all around us are tanks and gun emplacements; overhead is the entire United States Air Force. All bent on attacking me. We may surely feel with Job that there is a degree of overkill.

And then, not only has God attacked him. He has made sure Job is completely alone when attacked. There is no-one else in the tent. And so in verses 13–20 Job laments his isolation.

The monster god has isolated me cruelly (19:13–22)

This is a pathetic picture of the isolation of the sufferer. Alienated, estranged (verse 13), forgotten (verse 14). (We might imagine them saying, 'There is no point sending Job a Christmas card: he's as good as dead.') He is a stranger, an alien (verse 15) (even his wife cannot stand being near him); he is loathsome to his family (verse 17) and ridiculed (verse 18). The children coming back from school pause only to throw rotten fruit at him and stick out their tongues. And he is detested (verse 19). And then he sums it up in verses 21–22:

> Have mercy [pity] on me, have mercy on me, O you my friends,
>   for the hand of God has touched me!
> Why do you, like God, pursue me?

'Is God for me? Clearly not. This god is a monster, a fire-breathing dragon, a bully of the first order.' He picks on Job. He isolates him and he tears viciously at his life.

But we ought to pause a moment before we look at verses 23–27. For in verse 21 Job has said, *the hand of God has touched me.* Is it true that the hand of God has touched him? Let us look back at something we know but Job does not. We look back at 1:11–12, where Satan says to the Lord, *stretch out your hand and touch all that he has* . . . But the Lord does not stretch out his hand against Job. Instead in verse 12 we read, *And the* LORD *said to Satan, 'Behold, all that he has is in your hand.'* Again in 2:5–6 Satan asks the Lord to *stretch out your hand* . . . but the Lord replies, *Behold, he is in your hand* . . . The hands and fingers that destroyed Job's possessions and killed Job's children and wrecked Job's health were the hands of Satan, not the hands of God. Certainly this is the hand of Satan acting with the permission of the Lord and within the strict constraints given by the Lord; but it was Satan's hand and not God's that actually did these terrible things. And this is very important. For whose are the monstrous hands that have attacked Job and ripped at him and isolated him and made his life a misery? Answer: the hands of the enemy, Satan – acting with the permission of God and constrained by the strict limits given by God.

We shall see in later sections that this is a vital insight. Again and again, Satan masquerades as God and persuades Job that it is directly the Lord who has turned against him. As when the Roman soldiers blindfolded Jesus, hit him and asked, *Who is it that struck you?* (Luke 22:64), Job cannot see whose hand is striking him. We know this, but Job does not and his friends certainly do not. We saw in chapter 4 that the friends have no place in their theology for Satan. Their world is a simple slot-machine world, with one slot-machine maker who has set the rules: put in a coin of goodness and out pops a canister of blessing; put in a coin of badness, out clunks a parcel of poison. Their god is not the Creator and Sustainer, but the clockmaker who sets the machine running and then just leaves it to run (an idea later shared by the eighteenth-century deists at the time of the Enlightenment). The idea that there might be real forces of evil in this world, forces with real personality and real influence, has no place in their thinking.

But although Job, like his friends, does not know what has happened in heaven (Job 1 – 2), he is now beginning to wonder whose hand is behind his suffering. We have seen how in 9:24 he asks in perplexity, *if it is not he* [the Lord], *who then is it* who treats his world so unfairly? These things are happening and God is in control, so presumably they are God's doing, are they not? For if it is not God doing them, who is it?

For although most of Job's laments are just that – laments – somehow Job as a real believer cannot let go of the hope that ultimately the monster god is not the true God who has the last word. We find this longing hinted at in 9:33–35:

> *There is no arbiter between us* [me and God],
> *who might lay his hand on us both*
> (verse 33)

Or this may be translated, *Would that there were an arbiter . . .* However it is translated, the sense is that he wishes there were an arbiter, a just judge who would see that justice is done, as it were a God above and beyond the monster god.

In 16:18–21 we see this longing grow stronger. *O earth, cover not my blood* – that is to say, may my innocence and the unfairness of it all never be forgotten (like the blood of *righteous* Abel in Genesis 4:10). May it not be that an innocent man be quietly buried and forgotten.

> *let my cry* [for justice] *find no resting-place.*
> *Even now, behold, my witness* [who speaks up for me in the court]
> *is in heaven, and he who testifies for me is on high.*
> (16:18–19)

Somehow Job glimpses that there is justice in the end, that a real believer will finally be vindicated and seen to be a real believer.

And so in the latter part of Job 19 we reach perhaps the pinnacle of Job's faith in the darkness.

The Redeemer God (19:25–27)

In 19:23–24 Job is still glum. He has been fighting to prove his innocence, but it is a losing battle. He is pretty sure he is going to die. And he knows (verse 22b) that when he dies, his friends will not be satisfied with his death. No, they must also malign his reputation forever. They will put on his gravestone, 'Here lies Job, who was a sinner with secret sins he refused to confess; he has paid the penalty for his sins at last and the justice of God has been vindicated by his death. May he not rest in peace.'

And so in verses 23–24 Job simply longs that his protestations of innocence may be recorded permanently *in a book* (a nice irony), or (verse 24) *engraved in the rock*: inscribed on a memorial that cannot be erased. But then in verse 25, looking forward to that time after his death, he says:

> *For I know that my Redeemer lives,*
> *and at the last he will stand upon the earth.*

The word 'earth' may be translated as 'dust', the Lord perhaps standing over Job's grave as a living testimony – better than the dead words of a written memorial.

We are unsure of the exact meaning of verse 26 (in particular whether Job is expecting something 'in my flesh' or 'without my flesh'), but it seems that after his death Job expects that he himself will see God (verse 27). The Hebrew word translated 'Redeemer' often means someone to whom one is related, someone who is in some way kin or family, whose job it is to make sure that justice is done for a fellow family member. For example, in the Old Testament books we sometimes come across the so-called 'avenger of blood' whose job it was (in the days before law courts) to make sure justice was done when a member of his family was murdered. This is the same word translated here 'Redeemer'. We find a related idea in the book of Ruth where Boaz acts as Ruth's kinsman-redeemer, caring for her in her widowhood and in fact becoming for her the husband she needs.

So Job says, in effect, 'I will not finally believe that the monster god is the God who made this world. For I know that the God I have always feared and loved, this God is related to me by covenant – I belong to him and his family and his people – and in the end, even if it is after my death, I shall see him and he will vindicate me so that it will be publicly seen that I have been a real believer with a clear conscience.'

So who is this Redeemer? Surely it is the living God himself. No wonder at the end of verse 27 Job is deeply moved: *My heart faints within me!* More literally, 'How my bowels fail within me' with such deep longing. For in Hebrew the heart is not the seat of the emotions. In the Old Testament we do not feel with the heart; we feel with the bowels. Rather as we might say, 'I had butterflies in my stomach' – only much stronger. In the depth of his suffering Job says, 'I know that one day I shall see the living God who will vindicate me.' And the prospect touches him so deeply he trembles with terrified longing.

How may we be sure this is not wishful thinking? In Handel's *Messiah* there is a famous soprano aria in which Handel puts Job 19:25–26 alongside 1 Corinthians 15:20:

> I know that my Redeemer liveth,
>> and that he shall stand at the latter day upon the earth.
> And though worms destroy this body,
>> yet in my flesh I shall see God.
> For now is Christ risen from the dead,
>> the first-fruits of them that sleep.

This is deeply perceptive. The reason we know that Job's confidence is not wishful thinking is because Christ was raised. There was once a real believer whom the monster god attacked with all his vicious terrors; a blameless believer done to a terrible death he did not deserve. And the Redeemer God publicly vindicated him on the third day when he raised him from the dead. And so the bodily resurrection of Christ gives us the assurance that Job's confidence here was not wishful make-believe, but a sure hope.

This is an extraordinary insight of faith. Even though Job then goes back into further chapters of lament, Christians read these words and rightly say, 'How Job spoke more truly than he realized!' There is a sovereign Redeemer who lives and who will one day vindicate every believer and declare him and her justified from all sin. The true God is the Father who sent his Son into the world to be the innocent believer who dies for sinners; and the true God is the Son who so loved us that he gave himself for us. And so indeed every believer may say, 'God is for me in Christ; and no power or death or demon in the present or the future can separate me from his love in Christ' (Romans 8:38–39).

Each of us who suffers or who cares for another who suffers, must ask, 'Why? Why has this happened? Why did this happen to me or to her or him?' And we ask, perhaps in some desperation, 'Is God for me or against me?' Because it sometimes feels as though God is a monster out to make life a misery, so that we, or one for whom we care, may feel very alone and hurt very deeply. As we hear Job's faith in these words, we can bring our pain to the Lord Jesus Christ. Even though our life may be ebbing away and our wick burning low, we too may say:

> *I know that my Redeemer lives,*
> > *and at the last he will stand upon the earth.*
> *And after my skin has been thus destroyed,*
> > *yet in my flesh I shall see God,*
> *whom I shall see for myself,*
> > *and my eyes shall behold, and not another.*
> > *My heart faints within me!*
>
> (Job 19:25–28)

7 Why will God not answer my question? (Job 28)

Job has screamed out an urgent existential question: Why? (1:20, 23). This is not the question of the armchair religious or philosophical dilettante, enjoying a titillating debate. This is the agonized question of the 'wheelchair' sufferer who feels he or she needs desperately to know the answer. In Job 28 we stand back from the pain and the debates to ask why God will not answer the question 'Why?'

For despite the wonderful glimpse of faith in chapter 19, with which we closed the last chapter, the debates of Job with his friends have continued to flow to and fro. And by the start of Job 28 we may be forgiven for wondering if these hot debates are getting anywhere at all. For the best part of three cycles of speeches Job's friends have disputed with Job. In this short introduction we have had to confine ourselves to seeking the big themes and motifs, both in the theology of Job's comforters (chapter 4) and the struggles of Job (chapters 5 – 6). But round and round they have all gone, with a great deal of repetition in argument and an increasing heatedness of tone. The third cycle begins (as do the other two cycles) with Eliphaz (Job 22), answered by Job in Job 23 and 24. Then, with uncharacteristic brevity Bildad splutters and shuts up in Job 25 (just six verses), and Job replies. But Zophar never gets a third speech. The cycles do not end tidily, but seem to peter out as the barrage of words dies away into an embarrassed silence.

So before Job 28 we have this ragged end to the cycles of speeches. After Job 28, Job makes his final statement for the defence (Job 29 – 31), and we shall consider this in the next chapter. In between, Job 28 stands on its own. The ESV assumes (with its heading 'Job Continues: Where Is Wisdom?') that this is still Job speaking. Certainly there is no new heading in the Hebrew text, and this may still be Job. Alternatively it may be an interlude, a poem inserted by the narrator. But whoever is the poet at this point, Job 28 is a very different chapter from those that surround it. It has no smooth connection with the immediate contexts before or after; it is not addressed to any of the participants; it contains no accusations, no complaints and no responses to anything said previously. And it has a reflective tone that contrasts with the passionate arguments on either side. Here is a tranquil, contemplative pause for thought. If Job were read aloud, this chapter would be read in a quieter tone of voice. In a Greek tragedy it might be read by a chorus standing at the back of the stage. So in this section we consider this wonderful poem and how it contributes to our understanding of the person of Job, the book of Job, the world of Job and, above all, the God of Job.

A costly search for a valuable object (28:1–11)

The poem begins, with no explanation, by inviting us to tour around and marvel at the wonders of human mining exploration. Two motifs interweave: on the one hand an object of great value; on the other a search of great difficulty and cost. 'Think about the miner,' says our poet. 'He has an immensely dangerous and difficult task. But it is worth it, for the objects of his search are of such wonderful value.'

As we read it, we note all sorts of ways in which this poem prompts us to make links with the drama of the book:

> Surely there is a mine for silver,
>> and a place for gold that they refine.
> Iron is taken out of the earth,
>> and copper is smelted from the ore.

Man puts an end to darkness
  and searches out to the farthest limit
  the ore in gloom and deep darkness.
He opens shafts in a valley away from where anyone lives;
  they [the miners] *are forgotten by travellers;*
  they hang in the air, far away from mankind; they swing to and fro
    [perhaps from ropes or in cages while working in a vertical shaft].
As for the earth, out of it comes bread,
  but underneath it is turned up as by fire.
Its stones are the place of sapphires,
  and it has dust of gold.

That path no bird of prey knows,
  and the falcon's eye has not seen it.
The proud beasts have not trodden it;
  the lion has not passed over it.
Man puts his hand to the flinty rock
  and overturns mountains by the roots.
He cuts out channels in the rocks,
  and his eye sees every precious thing.
He dams up the streams so that they do not trickle,
  and the thing that is hidden he brings out to light.
(Job 28:1–11)

The *mine* (verse 1a) is a deep, mysterious place. We are immediately drawn into a world with puzzles and hidden perplexities, things we cannot find and cannot understand, and yet that are of value, worth searching out. And yet these valuable things have been placed here (verse 1, *a place*), which obliquely suggests that just maybe someone has deliberately placed these valuable things in such a way that they are hard to find. And yet it is so worth finding; which reminds us of Job's longing, *Oh, that I knew where I might find him* [God] (23:3). This search is dangerous, lonely and difficult (verse 4), for these precious jewels are not easily found or extracted. So also Job himself is not just suffering; he is searching desperately and in great loneliness to understand the answer to the question 'Why?'

Whereas agriculture is relatively easy (verse 5a), the search for this hidden treasure is hard and violent (verses 5b, 9). This is no light or airy matter, a matter of casual interest. Here (verses 7–8) is a search characteristic of humankind alone. Neither the falcon with his matchless eyesight nor the lion with his unparalleled strength is engaged in this particular costly search. So the poet has drawn us into a search. It is a search for something of matchless value, a search only embarked upon by those prepared for pain and loneliness, and therefore by those (human beings) who truly appreciate the matchless value of the object of the search.

Why has he drawn us into this search and caused us to meditate upon its necessity and its cost? He answers that in verse 12.

Here, in the poem about mining, is a parallel in the natural domain with a greater and deeper search in the cosmic domain, the search for Wisdom. Wisdom (synonymous with Understanding) here is what we would call Wisdom with a capital 'W'. In the imagery of the Old Testament this Wisdom means something like the architecture of the universe:

> The LORD by wisdom founded the earth;
>> by understanding he established the heavens.
>
> (Proverbs 3:19)

When God built the universe, like a building, he did so according to the blueprint called Wisdom. Wisdom is the fundamental underlying Order according to which the universe is constructed. This is deeper than just an Order in its material composition (the subject of the study of the material sciences); for this Order extends also to the moral and spiritual dimensions of existence. It is metaphysical as well as physical. For the idea that this world might just have order in its material aspect (the subject of the physical sciences) but not in its moral aspect would be unthinkable to the ancient (or modern) believer. Just as the physical scientist pursues the project of science in the belief that there is order to be discovered (which is why so much of the modern scientific enterprise has roots in Christian soil), so the believer lives on this earth in the conviction that it is finally not a chaotic universe, but one built upon a fundamental underlying and majestic order. It is of course this conviction that is so sorely challenged in the life and experience of Job.

Sometimes we speak of the 'architecture' of a piece of hardware or software. And by this we mean the underlying structure, such that, if we understand it, we shall grasp why it behaves and responds as it does. In a similar way, the poet knows that if only we can grasp the architecture or structure of the universe, then we shall know the answer to the question 'Why?' (3:20, 23). And we shall know the answer not only for our personal pain, but also for every person and each event in history.

We might imagine that the book of Job is primarily about arguments and philosophies and debates. It is not: it is about the search of a believing sufferer for Wisdom, the longing to understand *why* this world is as it is. And implicit therefore in this as yet unexplained start to the poem is the invitation to us as readers to be not just philosophers, thinkers or debaters, but to be honest seekers after Wisdom.

And so the poet moves to a meditation on the most deeply frustrating tension of Job's existence. He simply must know the answer to the question 'Why?', and yet he cannot find this out.

Wisdom is priceless and unobtainable at the same time (28:12–22)

Two motifs interweave in verses 1–11. On the one hand, jewels are valuable (e.g. verse 10 'precious'); on the other, inaccessible. The poet now turns to Wisdom or Understanding (which are synonymous), and develops in parallel these two themes, value and inaccessibility.

In verses 15–19 he majors on its matchless value. But he brackets this praise with two parallel laments of its inaccessibility (12–14, 20–22). Here is something that cannot be found (12–14), and yet simply must be found if life is to be worth living (15–19); and yet it really cannot be found. This is the 'sandwich' structure of verses 12–22:

- 12–14: Wisdom cannot be found
- 15–19: Wisdom is so valuable that it simply must be found
- 20–22: Wisdom cannot be found

But where shall wisdom be found?
   And where is the place of understanding?
Man does not know its worth,
   and it is not found in the land of the living.
The deep says, 'It is not in me,'
   and the sea says, 'It is not with me.'
    It cannot be bought for gold,
      and silver cannot be weighed as its price.
    It cannot be valued in the gold of Ophir,
      in precious onyx or sapphire.
    Gold and glass cannot equal it,
      nor can it be exchanged for jewels of fine gold.
    No mention shall be made of coral or of crystal;
      the price of wisdom is above pearls.
    The topaz of Ethiopia cannot equal it,
      nor can it be valued in pure gold.
From where, then, does wisdom come?
   And where is the place of understanding?
It is hidden from the eyes of all living
   and concealed from the birds of the air.
Abaddon and Death say,
   'We have heard a rumour of it with our ears.'
Job 28:12–22

The incomparable value of Wisdom is spelled out with poetic vigour in verses 15–19. The poet wants us to be in no doubt of the priceless value of gaining a grasp of how this world fits together, how it works, what its foundational structure (moral, as well as material) is. And no-one so longs to grasp what this order is as the suffering believer.

If any search is worth pursuing, surely this is it. For wisdom lies, as it were, at the root of the whole created order, underpinning it, set in place before the world was made (see Proverbs 8:22–31). And if only Job, or any believer, can gain access to this understanding, then the question 'Why?' will be answered. Job will know why all this has happened to him. At last he will not be suffering in the dark. And so in verses 15–19 the poet piles up images of the most precious things this world affords. Pile up all the gold and silver, he implies (verse 15), the very best gold (verse 16a), onyx and sapphire (verse 16b), wonderful jewels, coral, crystal, topaz (verses 17–19). Collect together all the riches of the whole wide wonderful world, and still you will have insufficient wealth to purchase wisdom or gain access to this understanding for which you yearn.

Here, in the eloquent language of poetry, is motivation piled upon motivation to pursue this search. And yet we know from verses 12–14 that this search is bound to fail. For wisdom *is not found in the land of the living* (verse 13) and even if we were to venture into the *deep*, the lowest part of the sea, the place where, in the poetic cosmology, the entrances to the place of the dead were, even there our enquiries would be met with blank looks (verse 14). And so in verses 20–22 the poet dumps us back on the ash-heap of frustration. No, he says, this search that seemed so passionately worth pursuing, where does it end? It ends with lonely Job on his heap of rubbish screaming the question 'Why?' (1:20, 23). For no living creature can find wisdom (verse 21). And even were we to go to the guardians of the most desperate extremities of the cosmos, Destruction (Abaddon, the angel of the bottomless pit; cf. Revelation 9:11) and Death (verse 22), even these terrible personified powers would have to shrug their shoulders and say, 'Well, yes, if you press me, I think I did once hear a third-hand rumour that somewhere Wisdom exists. But I have no idea where to find it.'

What is the poet doing? He is giving us pause for thought. We have been caught up in an awesome and terrible human tension. Job longs to know why. Is he right to long to understand? Yes, he is. For to understand this would be to understand the radical structure of the universe, and no greater goal can be possible for the human seeker. O, yes, he is right to search. But is his search doomed to failure? Yes, it is. He must seek, and yet he will never find wisdom.

If the poem ended at verse 22 it would indeed be a theatre of the absurd, a poetry to breed despair and nurture the living death of nihilism. But it does not end in verse 22. And in verses 23–28 the poet offers us a paradoxical but profound resolution.

The humbling resolution (28:23–28)

With one voice the poet has sung the praises of wisdom and extolled the value of understanding. With a parallel voice he has lamented the utter inaccessibility of wisdom. Twice he has asked:

But where shall wisdom be found?
  And where is the place of understanding?
(28:12)

From where, then, does wisdom come?
  And where is the place of understanding?
(28:20)

In verses 23–24 he almost answers himself, but not quite:

God understands the way to it,
  and he knows its place.
For he looks to the ends of the earth
  and sees everything under the heavens.

We are not told the location of wisdom, but our eyes are directed to the one who alone knows that *place* (verses 12, 20, linking back to verse 1b), for he has set it in place; and therefore he alone understands the way.

And in an anticipation of the Lord's speeches at the end of the book, the poet presses home his point by directing our wonder to one of the most uncontrollable and seemingly random facets of the created order: the weather!

When he gave to the wind its weight
  and apportioned the waters by measure,
when he made a decree for the rain
  and a way for the lightning of the thunder,
then he saw it and declared it;
  he established it, and searched it out.
(28:25–27)

Even today with supercomputers, satellites and a myriad of weather sensors, we struggle to make sense of the world's weather systems. Here is a wildly unpredictable and uncontrollable random force on the margins of the ordered world; here, breaking into our ordered lives day by day, is chaos and threat. And yet God

- *gave to the wind its weight* (told it when to blow hard and when soft)
- *apportioned the waters by measure* (told the flood and river waters and seas to go here but not there, to stop at this point; cf. 38:8–11)
- *made a decree for the rain* (telling it when, where and how much to fall)
- *made . . . a way for the lightning of the thunder* (controlled every rumble of thunder and each lightning flash)

And, says our poet, when God ordered the weather systems of the cosmos, he also *saw, declared, established* and *searched . . . out* wisdom (verse 27). The imagery may be of a skilled jeweller seeing a jewel (he *saw*), examining it (to *declare* its worth), preparing it (*establishing*) and probing it for flaws (*searched . . . out*). Wisdom is the centrepiece of God's 'Crown Jewels', utterly flawless and of infinite value. And God alone knows its place.

And there the poem ends. For verse 28 is a prose postscript not sharing the metre of verses 1–27. And as the poem ends it may be that our hopes are raised. For surely if God knows the way to wisdom, maybe he will take us there and open our eyes that we too may know everything and grasp wisdom and find the answers to all our agonized questions.

Not so! We have listened to the voices of the deep and the sea (verse 14), of Abaddon and Death (verse 22). Now let us listen to the voice of God. For verse 28 is the first time God has spoken in the book since the drama of Job 1 and 2, and the first time in the whole book that he has spoken to human beings:

And he said to man,
'Behold, the fear of the Lord, that is wisdom,
  and to turn away from evil is understanding.'

In a saying crucial to the whole book, God directs our attention away from our agonized questions and towards himself. He does not take us by the hand and lead us to the answers; rather, he beckons us to bow before the Lord himself, who knows the answers but chooses not to tell us. Our eyes are directed away from the search for the Architecture and towards the person of the Architect. We ask, 'Why doesn't God answer *my* question?' To which he replies, 'Turn your gaze and your enquiry away from the answer you want and towards the God you must seek. If you want to live in this world as a wise person, a man or woman of understanding, rather than a fool, do not seek Wisdom for its own sake. For if you were to find it you would become a puffed-up know-all (cf. 1 Corinthians 8:1). So do not seek Wisdom; seek the Lord.'

This is deeply humbling. Neither the marvels of human technology nor the insights of human philosophy yield the ultimate goal, the 'Theory of Everything'. And yet the truth of verse 28 is also profoundly reassuring. Right at the start we saw Job fearing God and turning away from evil (1:1). The heavenly courtroom knows that God approves of this (1:8; 2:3). But now Job himself, and every other human being, knows for sure that what Job was doing at the start is precisely what he ought to have been doing and it is what he – and we – ought to continue to do. We ought not to expect to find Wisdom (to know the answers to our questions) but rather to bow in humble worship before the One who does, and therefore to turn from evil.

There is, if we may put it like this, a distinction between Wisdom with a capital 'W' and wisdom with a small 'w'. Hebrew does not have this lower case / upper case distinction. But there is still a hint of difference in the original: in verses 12 and 20 'Wisdom' is written with the definite article (literally 'the Wisdom'), whereas in verse 28 it lacks this (simply 'wisdom'). And there does seem to be a distinction between the Wisdom and Understanding that are the subject of the poem (1–27) and the wisdom and understanding that are the calling of human beings in verse 28. To find the former would be to grasp the hidden order at the heart of the universe, whereas to find the latter is to live by faith not by sight, bowing before the Creator and looking to him alone.

What has this wonderful poem achieved? Before anything else it has made us stop to think. We must pause when we read this. Why this curious and seemingly irrelevant poem interrupting the passionate ebb and flow of debate? Answer: we must ponder and consider again the biggest issues of the book. What are the really big questions? And where have we got to in unravelling them? Not far! Indeed, Job 28 may be seen as implicit criticism of the sterile arguments of Job's three friends, whose speeches have achieved so little.

In this respect (and some others) Job 28 anticipates the speeches of God at the end of the book.

But why have we not made more progress? It is not only because Job's friends are foolish. At a deeper level, this poem teaches that although the questions Job asks are big and significant (Wisdom is indeed of priceless value), the search for Wisdom *as an object in itself* is doomed. The seeking required of us is not ultimately the seeking for philosophical answers or even for practical wisdom; it is the seeking after God himself. This is, we remember, one of the great marks we have noted of Job the believer. For while he cannot make head or tail of his perplexities, in his heart and with his voice he longs passionately for God. And in so doing, in continuing to fear God and turn from evil, he is precisely on the right track.

Job 28:28 gives divine affirmation to Job (and to us) that we need no secret of the higher life, no mysterious spiritual law to raise us to a deeper level of spirituality or godliness, no 'answers' achieved only by some spiritual elite. No, we are called, as was Job, to begin our lives of discipleship with the fear of God and repentance from evil, and to continue our walk with God in exactly the way we started it (cf. Colossians 2:6).

When the early Christians meditated and reflected on Jesus Christ, one of the Old Testament categories they found themselves drawn to was Wisdom. In his blameless life, his undeserved death and his vindication on the third day, Jesus Christ was and is the Wisdom of God, *Christ, in whom are hidden all the treasures of wisdom and knowledge* (Colossians 2:2–3). Jesus Christ himself was and is the wise man par excellence. He supremely, more even than Job, feared God and turned away from evil. And in his life and death and resurrection the fundamental structure of the universe, Wisdom, is revealed as in no other way. All the treasures of wisdom are to be found in him.

8   Why justification matters desperately (Job 29 – 31)

In a way, the book of Job might have ended at 28:28. Here, for the first time in the book, are words spoken by God to man (rather than spoken by God in the heavenly council):

> *Behold, the fear of the Lord, that is wisdom,*
>   *and to turn away from evil, that is understanding.*

Job has wanted God to speak; in 28:28 we are reminded that he has already spoken. We were told in 1:1, 1:8 and 2:3 that Job fears the Lord and turns from evil. Now God affirms that in so doing he is right and wise. It is not for mortal man to expect to find the answer to everything, to find Wisdom with a capital 'W'. No, our calling is to begin our lives of discipleship by bowing in humble fear before God, and to continue our walk in exactly the way we began. 'Never mind that there are puzzles: go on fearing God and turning from evil.' And there we might quite reasonably end. For there is a hint of closure in 28:28 with its link back to the beginning of the book: 'That's it; there are no answers, and we are not to expect any.' Except that in Job 29 – 31 Job launches into his last and arguably most eloquent and coherent speech of all, summing up for his defence.

So after our quiet pause for reflection in Job 28 we are plunged forcibly back to the rubbish heap where Job still sits, scratching his miserable plagued body and nursing his lonely soul. His final appeal begins (Job 29) with a wistful remembrance of life before disaster (cf. Job 1:1–5). It continues with another heart-rending lament (Job 30), strongly reminiscent of his initial lament in Job 3. And it ends (Job 31) with a passionate protestation of innocence and final electrifying appeal for justice. He begins with a sad reminiscence of the good old days when he was justified before God.

Job 29: the good old days when I was justified

Two motifs are interwoven in Job's reminiscence of the good old days in Job 29. On the one hand he lived in a right relationship with God; on the other, in his relations with his fellow men he lived out the image of God in which he had been made. Both in his religion (relationship with God) and his ethics (relationship with men) he was righteous or justified.

He begins, as is fitting, with his relationship with God (verses 2–6). The defining character of those *months of old* were that God *watched over* him (verse 2), God shone his light on Job's life (verse 3) even in times of darkness, when he knew in experience *the friendship of God* (verse 4) and the intimate harmonious presence of the Almighty with him (verse 5). His walk through this world was a walk with God. And so, unsurprisingly, it was a time of blessing, of *steps . . . washed with butter*, when even the rock poured out oil (verse 6). For this, surely, is what it means to be justified before God, to be righteous in God's sight. When Job looks back, it is this supremely he remembers with wistfulness and the loss of which he laments: not the blessing for its own sake, but the intimate walk in friendship with God.

But this idyllic memory is not (and can never be, for authentic biblical faith) a circumscribed memory of just 'me and God'. And so in verses 7–17 and again in verses 21–25 he recalls the righteousness he was able to express in his relations with his fellow men. For Job was not just a man who 'happened' to be rich and powerful. He was one who imaged and reflected in his life the character of the God who had given him riches and power. He lived, that is to say, as a man made in the image of God. For just as God is gracious and cares for the needy and suffering, so did Job express that care, delivering the poor who cried for help and the fatherless in their need (verse 12), rescuing those at the point of death and the widow in her pain (verse 13), acting as eyes to the blind and feet to the lame (verse 15), a father to the needy (verse 16) and a righteous judge to give justice to the oppressed (verse 17). So, not surprisingly, in those days he was treated with great respect and honour (verses 7–10, 21–25). For here is a man living as man ought to live. Here, in another age, is the ideal king (cf. Psalm 72).

And here is the Saviour. For we cannot read this memory of Job without ourselves remembering the one whom Job foreshadowed, who walked through this world in perfect harmony with his Father and who perfectly represented the love and faithfulness of his Father among men, causing the widow's heart to sing for joy (verse 13; cf. Luke 7:11–17), giving eyes to the blind and feet to the lame.

Job expected that being justified before God and living a life of outworked righteousness in this world, he would continue to be blessed. This, in Old Testament language, is the burden of verses 18–20:

> Then I thought, 'I shall die in my nest,
>   and I shall multiply my days as the sand . . .'
> (29:18)

'Well, yes, Job,' we say. 'When we read 1:1–5 we expected that too.' Or we ought to have expected that, in a well-run world. But it doesn't seem to be a well-run world. And so in chapter 30 Job moves to his final lament.

Job 30: Job's final lament

But now . . . (30:1). And so Job brings us right back to the problem with which the speeches began. Why is this righteous man, this man who is surely justified in the sight of God and man, why is he sitting alone in misery on the rubbish heap outside the city wall, destitute and childless? In chapter 30 Job takes us right back to the darkness of Job 3 in a lament replete with echoes of that utter hopelessness and desperation. And again, just as in Job 29, there are two interwoven motifs. In Job 29 it begins with his righteous walk with God and moves on to his respected life among people. In Job 30 it begins with his despised life among people (30:1–10) and goes on to root this in the enmity of God for him.

But now they laugh at me (30:1), these common people who used to look up to me and treat me with the greatest respect and gratitude (29:21–25). In the old days they always let Job have the last word (29:21), never dreaming of capping his words with some opinion of their own; now they do not even listen to him at all. 'Common riff-raff, no-good layabouts, people who are rightly on the despised margins of society, they laugh at me and spit at me,' laments Job (verses 1–10). And why? *Because God has loosed my cord and humbled me* . . . (verse 11), Job's life is imaged by a tent, whose cord being loosed, is flapping helplessly in the wind and on the point of collapse. The reason Job is alone, despised and rejected by men (verses 11b–15), miserable beyond belief (verses 16–18) is that *God has cast me into the mire* (verse 19), God has *turned cruel to me* (verse 21), God tosses him about.

Throughout this book, Job unwaveringly sees that the root question in his life, as any other human life, is justification. Is he walking through this world in right relationship with the God who made him? For if he is, then all is bound to be well (29:1–6), and if he is not, then there is no hope (e.g. 30:23). What he cannot reconcile (and this is the burden of Job 31) is how, when he leads a righteous life, God treats him as if he did not. He cannot understand how he, who genuinely fears God and turns from evil, is treated by God as though he did neither of these wise things.

It is this demonic divorce between life and religion against which Job protests. 'After all,' he says (30:25) 'in my life *I* wept for the one having a hard time and grieved over the one in need. And I did so because this is what I had thought was the character of the God I feared. But you, God, do not seem to be treating *me* at all the way I treated others. I thought the river of mercy was supposed to flow first from you to me and then out from me to others; but as far as I can make out I seem to have poured mercy out to others while you have poured poison into me. And frankly, I cannot understand it.' Or, to put it another way, when Job recounts his right use of power in 29:11–17, he is implicitly saying to God, 'I ruled well in the limited area of my dominion; why don't you rule well in yours?' This protest leads into Job's final appeal.

Job 31: the final appeal

In chapter 31 Job catalogues a list of sins he might have committed, and which, if he had committed without repenting, would quite justly have caused God to treat him as an enemy. But – and this is his point – in fact he has not committed these sins. (Not, we remember, that he claims sinless perfection, but rather, in New Testament terms, that he is genuinely a believer walking in the light with no unconfessed or unrepented sin.)

And so, in Job 31:35–37, we reach a moment of quite extraordinary dramatic tension, as this mortal throws down the gauntlet in the courtroom of the universe before the God of the universe:

> *Oh, that I had one to hear me!*
> *(Here is my signature! Let the Almighty answer me!)*
> *Oh, that I had the indictment written by my adversary!*
> (Job 31:35)

In courtroom language, Job has run out of patience. He has challenged his accuser to make his case in court (e.g. 13:22), and instead he has had to endure the tediously repetitive accusations of his supposed friends, none of which has hit the mark. So, he says at last, I lay down my final case for the defence. I append my signature and challenge the Almighty, no less, to answer me. If I am guilty, then I challenge him to punish me as I deserve, with death. And if he does not, well then, I will be declared righteous by default. And all the world will know that I have been falsely accused.

This is a moment of electrifying tension. In our human power structures, it is a moment of high drama when a prime minister or president is summoned to appear before a tribunal. Here it is as if the Creator of the universe is summoned to appear before what is, in effect, an impeachment tribunal. For, implies Job, God has treated me as guilty; and if in fact I am not guilty, then God stands guilty of injustice; and God must therefore resign his throne. The stakes in this challenge are higher than the destiny of one man. For if in fact Job is innocent, it seems to the assembled courtroom (and certainly to Job) that God must be guilty. This is the issue at stake with the suffering believer. This final appeal of Job (and especially 31:35) is a turning point in the book. It breaks us out of the fruitless cycle of speeches between Job and his friends. But, as we shall see in the next section, it does so in a surprising way.

9   A surprising new voice (Job 32 – 37)

At the end of Job 31 we could cut the atmosphere with a knife. With seeming brash insolence a mortal man has challenged God to prove that he, the mortal, is guilty as (implicitly) charged, when he claims he is not guilty. With the implication that if God cannot do this, or will not execute the necessary sentence of death, then God himself ought to resign because he is not running the world as he ought.

Job has demanded (31:35) that the Almighty should 'hear' him: give him the court hearing he requires. But the Almighty does not seem to be bothered to grant this hearing. It is rather as when King David seems to some to be getting a bit slack about his kingly duties, and his ambitious son Absalom goes to the city gate and wins the hearts of the people by whispering in their ears, *See, your claims are good and right, but there is no man designated by the king to* hear *you* (2 Samuel 15:3). So Satan whispers, 'The King is getting slack. He is not running his world as he ought. You ought to be granted a hearing, but unfortunately there is no-one around to deal with your case. Maybe – has the thought occurred to you? – maybe this 'King' you have served isn't such a good king after all.' Just so in our suffering we may indeed be lured away to doubt the goodness or sovereignty of God.

So what is going to happen? If we were God (what a dangerous thought!), we would surely be panicked by our predicament in this drama. We do seem to be in a corner. We have chosen to remain hidden off-stage, but now it seems that in spite of our claimed sovereignty we are going to be forced on stage to reveal our hand. Not at all! What actually happens is a complete surprise. The book enters its third and final major section, with the prose introduction of a completely new character.

It has been plausibly argued that the book consists of three major sections, each prefaced with a prose introduction of a new character or characters. So, the first section (1:1 – 2:10) began with the introduction of Job himself (1:1–5), and the second (2:11 – 31:40) with the introduction of his three friends (2:11–13). Now, in 32:1–5, the poetry of the previous 28 chapters pauses for the prose introduction of a young man called Elihu:

> *So these three men ceased to answer Job, because he was righteous in his own eyes. Then Elihu the son of Barachel the Buzite, of the family of Ram, burned with anger. He burned with anger at Job because he justified himself rather than God. He burned with anger also at Job's three friends because they had found no answer, although they had declared Job to be in the wrong. Now Elihu had waited to speak to Job because they were older than he. And when Elihu saw that there was no answer in the mouth of these three men, he burned with anger.*

The repetition of two words gives the key to what is happening here: *answer* and *anger*. Job has demanded (31:35) that the Almighty should answer him. The three friends have ceased to answer Job (verse 1), and their failure to answer him makes Elihu very angry (2, 5). This motif of answering is echoed many times in Elihu's speeches (e.g. 32:12, 14–17; 33:12).

And Elihu's anger is emphasized even more strongly in the Hebrew, where we meet his anger even before we hear his name (verse 2 begins literally, 'Then burned with anger Elihu . . .'); his anger is spoken of twice in verse 2, once in verse 3 and then again in verse 5. He is a very angry young man. Why is he so angry? He is angry because he correctly and accurately understands precisely the point with which we ended the last section, that the stakes are much higher than the suffering of one man. He is angry (verse 2) *because* [Job] *justified himself rather than God*: he made himself out to be righteous, which necessarily implies that God is not.

Before we dismiss his anger out of hand as the immaturity of youth, we need to understand that it was a defensible anger. Job is *righteous in his own eyes* (32:1) as the friends have realized (8:6; 11:4; 22:3) and as Job himself has made clear (e.g. 27:1–6). And instinctively, when we hear this we side with Elihu and the three friends. For we know from the teaching of Jesus that self-righteousness is offensive to God. In Luke 18:9–14 it is the penitent tax-collector who goes home justified in the sight of God, not the self-righteous Pharisee. So we need to remind ourselves that, contrary to our instincts, the book of Job has repeatedly told us that when *Job* affirms his righteousness (his right standing before God) he is correct to do so (1:1, 8; 2:3). And yet, even so, we can hardly help sympathizing with poor Elihu, who is so well motivated to defend the honour of God. He has heard God maligned as an evildoer, and he is livid, as indeed he ought to be. This is not an immature anger, but a defensible and godly anger, even if – as we know but he does not – this anger turns out to be misdirected.

Further, Job has summoned God himself to appear in court as his accuser. Elihu thinks this is outrageous. It is unthinkable that the living God should appear before a human, or even a cosmic, court. So he takes it upon himself to answer Job on God's behalf. Elihu therefore offers an answer to Job. He is going to speak as a prophet speaks, on behalf of God, to answer the accusations of Job. Elihu makes four speeches:

- 32:6 – 33:33 *And Elihu the son of Barachel the Buzite answered and said . . .*
- 34:1–37 *Then Elihu answered and said . . .*
- 35:1–16 *Then Elihu answered and said . . .*
- 36:1 – 37:24 *And Elihu continued, and said . . .*

Ought we to listen to Elihu?

It is common to write Elihu off lightly, for two reasons. First, he seems to us to be wordy and repetitive. Second, the Lord completely ignores him; he is not mentioned in the rest of the book at all. However, we need to be cautious. For the accusation that Elihu is a blustering, wordy young man is a subjective and cultural judgment (a judgment we might also wish to make about a number of authoritative prophetic texts); that we think him repetitive may reflect more on our impatience than on his inadequacy. It is true that at some points he does appear to us as rather self-centred (e.g. 32:10) and that he is sometimes harsh with Job (e.g. 34:36), but it may be an overreaction just to write him off as a distraction who fails to move the book forward.

And the fact that he is not mentioned later is inconclusive. For while the three friends are explicitly dismissed by God (42:7), Elihu is not. Do we conclude that God ignores him because he is irrelevant, or that God does not condemn him because he has made a worthwhile contribution to the book? There are suggestions in the text that he may be rather significant. He is dignified with something of a family tree (32:2), which is more than can be said for the three friends (2:11), and he is allotted four uninterrupted speeches, which is more than any of the three friends were allowed. Furthermore, unlike the three friends, Elihu engages rather carefully with what Job has said (e.g. quoting or summarizing Job's arguments in 33:9–11; 34:5–6; and 35:2–3).

So perhaps we ought to attend to Elihu rather more positively than has been common among commentators. For he may function as a constructive forerunner to the speeches of God himself that follow: he is not authoritative but he speaks with greater insight than the friends.

Elihu's first speech (32:6 – 33:33)

The core of Elihu's argument in his first speech lies in 33:8–30. He has begun the speech by defending his decision to speak at all (32:6–22) and encourages Job that he speaks 'from alongside' as a fellow human being (33:1–7); Job has no need to be terrified of Elihu (as he is of God; e.g. 9:14ff.; 13:21).

In Job 33:8–11 Elihu fairly accurately summarizes Job's position, which is that God has become his enemy for no good reason. Further, Job objects that God will not answer him (verse 13). On the contrary, says Elihu (verse 14), God does speak repeatedly (the idiom *in one way, and in two* has this sense of God's determination to get through by repetition; cf. verse 29 and Psalm 62:11). He speaks to us, whether or not we will listen (verse 14b). Sometimes he does so in a dream or some other means of getting through with deep conviction of sin to our minds and hearts (15–16). Why does he make us feel so bad about ourselves in this way? In order that we may repent, not become proud and so be rescued from death (17–18). God does speak, and when he does, it greatly disturbs us (verse 16, *terrifies*), but it is meant for our good.

But sometimes he speaks to us through pain (verses 19–28).

The precise imagery of verses 23–24 is not clear, but the main idea of the passage seems to be this. A man is sick (verses 19–22), but God has mercy on him and commands the angel of death to bring him back from his journey to death (verses 23–24). There is a ransom found for him, a sacrifice to pay the penalty for his sin. He is restored to health (verse 25) and to joy in right relation with God (verse 26) and publicly affirms God's goodness to him (verses 27–28). So his sickness proves to be a 'Severe Mercy' (in C. S. Lewis's haunting phrase), by which God has effectively spoken to him in order to rescue him from the pit (verses 28, 30).

Elihu's point is much the same as that made in the often-quoted section of C. S. Lewis's book *The Problem of Pain*:

> The human spirit will not even begin to try to surrender self-will as long as all seems to be well with it. Error and sin both have this property, that the deeper they are the less their victim suspects their existence; they are masked evil. Pain is unmasked, unmistakable evil; every man knows that something is wrong when he is being hurt . . . We can rest contentedly in our sins . . . But pain insists upon being attended to. God whispers to us in our pleasures, speaks in our conscience, but shouts in our pains: it is His megaphone to rouse a deaf world.[1]

We can see that Elihu has moved forward significantly from Job's friends in a number of ways. He listens carefully to what Job has actually said, and engages with him. He answers not with an impersonal system of rewards and punishments, but with a personal loving God who acts to bring suffering because he knows it is the only way to achieve the final good of rescuing a man. And yet we still find ourselves saying that, wise and perceptive as Elihu may be in places, his words are not directed at the right person. For while what he affirms here may be true, it is not the reason why God has afflicted Job (as we know from Job 1 and 2).

Elihu's second speech (Job 34)

This impression that Elihu is not going to provide us with the answer we need is strengthened when we read his second speech, which is less nuanced than the first and more full of indignation. In verses 5 and 6 he accurately summarizes Job's complaint that, although he is in the right, God has taken away his right (denied him justice). But in verses 7–9 Elihu more or less echoes the three friends when he accuses Job of keeping company with evildoers and walking with wicked men. The argument of Job 34 is that God is both absolutely sovereign and absolutely just, and therefore Job's complaint must be totally wrong. He even ends (verses 36–37) by wishing that Job were *tried to the end* because of his wicked answers which show that not only is he a sinner, but he is also a rebel against God. In this second speech Elihu is close to the spirit and the arguments of the three friends.

Elihu's third speech (Job 35)

It is not easy to distil Elihu's argument in his third speech. One important argument concerns the silence of God. Job has complained that God has not answered him and Job waits in vain for his case to be heard. 'That is not surprising,' says Elihu. 'For why should the great and transcendent God be bothered to answer a mere mortal, and a sinful one at that?' This is seen most clearly in verses 12–14:

> There they cry out, but he does not answer,
>> because of the pride of evil men.
> Surely God does not hear an empty cry,
>> nor does the Almighty regard it.
> How much less when you say that you do not see him,
>> that the case is before him, and you are waiting for him!

What are we to make of this? It seems heartless and lacking compassion to imply that God is too great to be bothered with the cry of an impudent, suffering mortal like Job. And yet, for all the inadequacy of Elihu's picture of an uncaring transcendent deity, as Elihu warms to his theme of the greatness of God we detect also the introduction of a theme that will reach its magnificent climax in God's own speeches.

Elihu's fourth speech (Job 36 – 37)

After repeating some of the previous arguments, from 36:22 onwards Elihu, using language of the storm, speaks mainly of the grandeur of God the Creator. Perhaps we are to imagine a massive thunderstorm breaking as Elihu speaks. If in Job 33 he says God speaks in dreams and in sickness, in Job 36 – 37 he speaks in the storm:

> Keep listening to the thunder of his voice
>   and the rumbling that comes from his mouth.
> (37:2)

Indeed Job 37 is a magnificent description of an awesome God revealed in a fearsome storm, with *whirlwind* included (37:9). Here is the God who is *great in power* and who will not violate justice (37:23); and therefore the proper response is to *fear him* (37:24), which is exactly the conclusion of the poem in Job 28 (28:28).

And it is *out of the whirlwind* that the Lord speaks (38:1). So there is a close link between the conclusion of Elihu's speeches and the Lord's speeches that follow.

What are we to make of Elihu?

It is difficult to know what we are to make of Elihu and his four speeches. Why does God give us these speeches without giving us a clear indication as to whether they are to be attended to or rejected? After all, usually in Scripture we have a pretty clear indication of how we are to treat a passage or saying. For example, when the prophets tell Jehoshaphat to go up in battle against Ramoth-Gilead (1 Kings 22:6), it becomes clear that these are false prophets, who are to be rejected. But in a few places in Scripture, it is much less clear. Elihu is one; parts of the book of Ecclesiastes are another.

The answer goes to the heart of wisdom: godly wisdom is not so much a word spoken to the human heart from the outside, as a character formed in the believer by the Spirit of God working by the Word of God at the deepest level of the human heart. In setting before us in Job these speeches in which truth and error are mixed, God invites us to think for ourselves, to puzzle, to engage with the process of wisdom fashioning our minds and hearts. There is an aspect of the Word of God that comes authoritatively to us from above, from the mountaintop of Sinai; this is the Law of God. But there is also an aspect of the Word of God that gets under our skin and into our soul and beavers away within us as we meditate, puzzle and think about the world and our place in it. This latter facet of the Word of God does not respond to the immature request to 'Tell me the answer'; rather it draws the seeking and searching believer into a lifelong process of wondering and prayerful meditation on God's Word.

Elihu may be a type of the puzzled believer, mixed both in motives and tone, mixed also in theology, and yet set before us as one who is on the way to wisdom. In his speeches there are valuable preparatory foreshadowings of the divine speeches that immediately follow. We do well not simply to write Elihu off as a misguided fool. He is not a prophet, speaking accurately for God; but neither is he a false prophet to be utterly condemned. But whatever Elihu is, and however we respond to his speeches, we are driven on from them towards the climax of the whole magnificent book, which is the subject of the next chapter.

Notes

1. C. S. Lewis, *The Problem of Pain* (London, 1940), pp. 80–81.

10   The God who is God (Job 38:1 – 42:6)

There is a contradiction in popular ideas about God in Britain. In 2004 the BBC world survey of attitudes to religion showed that the statement 'I find it hard to believe in God when there is so much suffering in the world' commanded the highest agreement rate in the UK, of all the countries polled. And yet the statement 'God could prevent suffering if he wanted to' commanded the lowest agreement rate in the UK, of all the countries polled.[1]

So while we find it hard to believe in God because of suffering, at the same time we feel that God, even if he does exist, probably could not do much about suffering if he tried. If we believe in any kind of God, he seems not to be a very strong God. This perhaps explains why 37% of the British survey reckoned that David Beckham is more influential in the world today than God. The issue in the Lord's magnificent speeches is, 'How strong is God?' And in particular it is the question 'Is he strong enough to control evil and keep it on a leash?'

We have watched Job, a real believer with a clear conscience, who fears God and turns away from evil. We have seen him as disaster after disaster struck with numbing ferocity. His possessions are destroyed, his children killed, his health disintegrates, and he is left alone in terrible suffering. And as he sits alone he cries out (3:20, 23), 'Why? Why does this happen? Why to me, and why to others also? Why? What is the answer? Is there an answer?'

Job longs to speak to God. He wants to appeal to the supreme judge in the supreme court of the universe. His friend Eliphaz thinks this is pointless:

> Call now; is there anyone who will answer you?
>   To which of the holy ones [members of the heavenly council] will you turn?
> (5:1)

Elihu also does not think there is much point in this search (37:23). And yet Job longs to speak to God. Wrung from the core of a troubled heart is the cry

> Oh, that I knew where I might find him,
>   that I might come even to his seat!
> (23:3)

'I want to speak to God and to hear what answer he has to my question' is the longing of Job.

We – the readers of the book of Job – have some idea of the answer to Job's question 'Why?' For we have listened in to two meetings of the heavenly courtroom or council chamber. Job has not. So, is *his* question going to be answered? Will the judge in charge of the supreme court speak to *him*? His friends have failed to answer him satisfactorily. Elihu has tried. But before there is any opportunity for Job or the three friends to respond to Elihu, there is the most magnificent interruption.

The Lord's first speech and Job's response (38:1 – 40:5)

> Then the LORD answered Job out of the whirlwind and said:
> 'Who is this that darkens counsel by words without knowledge?
> Dress for action like a man;
>   I will question you, and you make it known to me.'
> (38:1–2)

THE GOD WHO IS GOD | 91

Immediately the tables are turned and it is clear who is questioning whom. Although this is the Lord's *answer* to Job, it turns out to be an answer that consists mostly of questions. Job has wished he could summon the Lord into the courtroom. But the Lord summons Job.

This first speech contains some of the most beautiful nature poetry in human literature. 'Look around, Job; look around at a wonderful world. Look at the stars, the clouds, the waters, the land, the wild creatures, the funny ostrich, the war-horse, the eagle. Are *you* God? Did *you* make these? Because if you are God, then I'll happily resign and hand over the running of the universe to you [as happened, humorously, in the film *Bruce Almighty*]. But you're not, are you? So what makes you think you could run it better than me?'

This is the pervading sense of this speech. One core question in the book has been whether or not the cosmos is properly run, whether or not the God in charge deserves to be in charge, or whether perhaps he ought to be sacked or impeached for running it badly. And so the answer focuses also on God as the Creator who *laid the foundation of the earth* (38:4) and who put the whole thing together. And the emphasis is on the *whole* cosmos, including its extremities (e.g. 38:16–17). Job did not create the world and therefore Job does not understand how it all fits together, how it is structured and how it works. (There is a strong echo here of the logic of the poem of Job 28 with its humbling conclusion in verse 28.)

Shortly before Clement Attlee won a landslide victory in the British General Election of 1945, he had a lot of trouble from the Chairman of the Labour Party, one Professor Harold Laski. Apparently Laski kept writing to Attlee telling him how to do his job, or that he ought to resign. Attlee ended his reply to one of these tiresome letters with the pointed words 'a period of silence from you would now be most welcome'. God sometimes wants to say that to us, as he did here to Job: 'My Dear Job, thank you for all your 20 chapters worth of letters telling me how to run the world and suggesting I could do it better than I am. A period of silence from you would now be most welcome.'

And Job gets the message. He is utterly awed. 'Oh, yes, I'll shut up. In the presence of the Creator of the world, I'll shut my big mouth' (40:3–5).

But does God's speech answer Job's question? For the question is, 'Why do I, Job, who do not deserve it, suffer as I do?' The answer so far seems to be, 'Look around and you will understand that I the Lord am the Creator and sustainer of life, I am in control of all the world, and therefore you may trust me with your life and your un-answered questions.' Is this an answer? Well, yes and no.

Of course, we know Job has always been a true worshipper. He has never denied that the Lord is God, really God, in control, supreme, sovereign, all-powerful. And yet somehow this first speech forces him to look around and admit that the Lord really is God, who made and who sustains *all* the created order. And as the Lord speaks this word to him, he bows down deeper than ever and somehow his questions may be left safely at the feet of this Almighty God.

And yet there is still a problem. And this is something Christians always face when we say, in the words of that classic Louis Armstrong song, 'What a wonderful world'. The problem is this: yes, it is a won-derful world, and yet it is a world touched by terrible evil. It is a world where a cultured man may listen to Mozart while being commandant of an extermination camp at Belsen or Ravensbruck, a world where the beauty of sex may be twisted into infidelity and abuse, a world where the wonder of man's technological wizardry is used in the service of mass destruction. And it is a world in which blameless Job suffers.

And so the puzzle is this: what about the evil in the world? It is all very well for the Lord to be the good Creator of a good world. But what about the world we actually have to live in, a good world touched by darkness and death? Because this is the world we have to live in. It is the world Job lives in. It is the world any honest believer lives in. A world with pain, injustice, perplexity and sorrow. What about that world, the real world?

There has been a hint of an answer in the first speech.

> Or who shut in the sea with doors
>   when it burst out from the womb,
> when I made clouds its garment
>   and thick darkness its swaddling band,
> and prescribed limits for it
>   and set bars and doors,
> and said, 'Thus far shall you come, and no farther;
>   and here shall your proud waves be stayed'?
> (38:8–11)

In biblical imagery the sea, the raging water, is the place of threat and chaos and hostility to the security of the people of God (cf. Psalm 46:1–3). In the poetry of 38:8–11 the sea bursts out like an unruly and precocious newborn child from the womb. But it does not cover the whole earth. No, the Creator fixes limits – *Thus far . . . and no farther.* So there is a hint here that evil is restrained. But this hint is not developed until the second speech. For the second divine speech picks up on this objection that the problem of evil has not been adequately addressed.

The Lord's second speech and Job's response (40:6 – 42:6)

My mind [was] paralysed by the dreadful shape which had sprung out upon us from the shadows of the fog. A hound it was, an enormous coal-black hound, but not such a hound as mortal eyes have ever seen. Fire burst from its open mouth, its eyes glowed with a smouldering glare, its muzzle and hackles and dewlap were outlined in flickering flame. Never in the delirious dream of a disordered brain could anything more savage, more appalling, more hellish be conceived than that dark form and savage face which broke upon us out of the wall of fog.

You may remember that description by Arthur Conan-Doyle from *The Hound of the Baskervilles.*[2] The Hound of the Baskervilles turned out to have a natural explanation, albeit a surprising one. But in Job 41 we meet a hellish beast of real supernatural power.

In Job 40:15–24 we meet a land beast called Behemoth, and in Job 41 a water beast called Leviathan. What are they? Many commentaries tell us that Behemoth is probably the hippopotamus and Leviathan the crocodile (cf. NIV and ESV footnotes). And certainly there are elements of each in the descriptions. Other suggestions have been made identifying Behemoth and Leviathan with other real creatures. If this is the case, then Job 40 and 41 are a simple extension of the first speech. In the first speech Job is asked if, for example, he gives the horse his strength (39:19); now the Lord asks him if he can tame a crocodile. The point is essentially the same.

And yet this does not quite seem to do justice to these beasts. For this second speech provokes an even stronger reaction of worship and penitence in Job than the first (cf. 42:1–6 with 40:3–5), and there is a sense in which the challenges of this second speech are climactic. And if all this second speech is saying is, 'Job, you haven't made a hippo or tamed a crocodile,' then it is a bit of an anticlimax. As the sceptic George Bernard Shaw says in one of his plays, 'God really has to do better in explaining the problem of evil than to say, "You can't make a hippopotamus, can you?"'[3]

So what are the Behemoth and the Leviathan? In the ancient world, as today, when you wanted to speak about the world you often did so in terms of stories or myths. And one of the stories that did the rounds was of some kind of dragon god or serpent god or sea-monster god who was the arch-enemy of the chief god in the pantheon. And in the old stories, all sorts of battles were fought between this monster god and other gods.

The background to these myths was always polytheistic: behind the visible world are all sorts of gods and goddesses. Now sometimes the Old Testament writers use the language of these myths to teach what is actually true about the one living God. Let us look at Leviathan. In Job's first lament (3:8) he asks those *who are ready to rouse up Leviathan* to curse the day of his birth. Everyone agrees that he is not talking about a crocodile here. No, to rouse Leviathan is to call upon the arch-enemy of God, the prince of darkness, to come and undo a part of God's creation. It is almost what we would call satanism, calling upon Satan to come and bring darkness. This is not just a crocodile in Job 3, and it seems likely that it is more than a crocodile in Job 41.

In Psalm 74, speaking of the God who rescues, the psalmist says:

> You divided the sea by your might;
>   you broke the heads of the sea monsters on the waters.
> You crushed the heads of Leviathan . . .
> (Psalm 74:13–14)

Again, this is more than a crocodile. Here is God's big enemy described in story language: and God wins. Isaiah uses similar story language to express the victory of God:

In that day the LORD with his hard and great and strong sword will punish
Leviathan the fleeing serpent, Leviathan the twisting serpent, and he will slay the
dragon that is in the sea. (Isaiah 27:1)

So it seems that Leviathan in biblical imagery is the arch-enemy of
God, the prince of the power of evil, Satan, the god of this world (as
Jesus calls him). Here is the embodiment of beastliness, of terror, of
undiluted evil. This second divine speech to Job is precisely addressing the problem of evil in the created order. This is clear in Job
40:7–14. Job has questioned God's justice (verse 8). So God challenges
him to do the job of the judge of all the earth – that is (verse 11), to
bring low the proud and (verse 12) to tread down the wicked. 'If you
can do that' (verse 14), says the Lord, 'then I will admit that you can
save yourself. But you can't.'

And so the figures of Behemoth and Leviathan come not as an
anticlimax but rather use the language of well-known stories to
make the point that only the Lord can keep evil on a leash. We
cannot be certain about the precise significance of Behemoth, but in
his scholarly work on Job, Bob Fyall has argued that there is reason to
believe this beast stands for the personified figure of Death (rather as
we sometimes portray Death as a hooded figure with a sickle, the
grim reaper).[4] But whatever Behemoth is, the major focus in the
Lord's speech is on Leviathan.

Job is challenged with warm irony, *Can you draw out Leviathan with
a fish-hook . . .?* (41:1). 'Go on, Job, have a go! Take your fly-fishing
line, tie a fly, cast it over the water, and when you've hooked
Leviathan, see if you can pull him in. Have a go!' The black humour
is like one of those disaster films where a fisherman sits on the end
of a wooden pier and hooks a whale or a great white shark, with
disastrous results.

And so the dark comic irony continues through verses 1–9: 'Why
don't you put him on a dog-lead and bring him home to tea? And
when your little daughters come to greet you, say to them,
"Darlings, I've brought you something you'll love, a sweet cosy pet;
come and look at it; it's called a Leviathan"' (verse 5b).

Then, with cruel comedy, we see the little girls swallowed up by
this terrible fire-breathing dragon. 'Of course you couldn't do that,
Job. The very idea is utterly absurd. Will you try to take on the power

of cosmic evil on your own? You won't forget the battle, and I rather doubt if you will want to challenge him again! Because you haven't a hope' (verse 8).

And then there is a surprise:

> No one is so fierce that he dares to stir him [Leviathan] up.
>> Who then is he who can stand before me?
> Who has first given to me, that I should repay him?
>> Whatever is under the whole heaven is mine.
>
> (41:10–11; my emphasis)

The Lord has sung the praise of Leviathan's terrifying strength. But why has he done so? Why has he filled Job's mind with the awesome terrors of evil? Answer: so that Job may understand that he, the Lord, is stronger still.

And then in verses 12–34 the Lord returns to a hymn of praise of the great strength of Leviathan, a supernaturally powerful beast. This hymn concludes:

> On earth there is not his like,
>> a creature without fear.
> He sees everything that is high;
>> he is king over all the sons of pride.
>
> (41:33–34)

That is, he is *the ruler of this world* (John 12:31), *the prince of the power of the air* (Ephesians 2:2). So here is a creature who is topmost of all the proud. 'If you can tame *him*, Job, well then we may be sure you can tame all the proud. But you can't, Job, can you?' Indeed we saw in Job 19 that it is precisely this monster who has been savaging Job and making his life such utter misery all this time. Job cannot take him on. The point of Job 41 is to make us tremble at the awesome and fell power of the prince of evil. If we thought evil was bad, when we come face to face with Leviathan we realize it is infinitely more frightening than we had thought. 'You cannot begin to take on the problem of evil, Job. And you know that.'

'But *I* can!' says the Lord. That is the point. This awesome monster is (verse 33) a *creature*, a created thing. 'I made him too, and I can tame him. And he is on *my* leash, even if he cannot be on yours' (see verse 5). (We see similar ironic comedy in Psalm 104:26 with its calm description of Leviathan as placed in the sea to frolic, as a parent might put an unruly child in a secure playpen to play.)

Now this is the point. A walker enters a farmyard and is terrified by wild dogs, yapping, snarling and snapping around his ankles. He is scared. And the question he is bound to ask is, 'Are these dogs restrained in any way? Are they on a lead? Is there an owner around who can call them off?' As Job suffers, his greatest and deepest fear is that the monster who attacks him is unrestrained, that the attacks will go on forever, with unrelieved ferocity, and that the monster has been given a free hand, unlimited access to Job and his life. He is afraid that there is no sovereign God who has evil on a leash.

But there is. And when Job grasps that, he is filled with awe (42:2). We, the readers, have already seen this in chapters 1 and 2, in which it is clear that Satan is restrained (1:12). On both occasions Satan obeys to the letter. Satan, Leviathan, is a horrible monster. But he cannot go one millimetre beyond the leash on which the Lord keeps him.

Now this does not answer our questions. It does not give us a philosophically filled in and tidied up schema that can explain the problem of suffering and evil. But it does something deeper: it opens our eyes to who God is. He is the only God, without rival. Even the mystery of evil is his mystery. Even Satan, the Leviathan, is God's Satan, God's pet – dare we put it like this. And that means that as we suffer, and as we sit with others who suffer, we may with absolute confidence bow down to this sovereign God, knowing that the evil that comes may be terrible, but it cannot and will not ever go one tiny fraction beyond the leash on which God has put it. And it will not go on forever. For the One to whom we belong is God.

It is not until the New Testament that we learn what it cost God to win this victory over Leviathan. For this was no Olympian victory won from a great height by an impassive dictator God. On the contrary, this victory was won, paradoxically, on the cross of Christ. As the writer of the letter to the Hebrews explains, the reason the Son of God became a fully human being was, *that through death he might destroy the one who has the power of death, that is, the devil* (Hebrews

2:14). The reason Leviathan the monster has a hold over human beings is that we have surrendered to his cruel sovereignty by rebellion against God; *the sting of death is sin* (1 Corinthians 15:56). We owe him our dark allegiance and cannot escape his clutches, until our debt is paid. That debt was paid at the cross:

> And you, who were dead in your trespasses and the uncircumcision of your flesh,
> God made alive together with him, having forgiven us all our trespasses, by cancelling
> the record of debt that stood against us with its legal demands. This he set aside,
> nailing it to the cross. He disarmed the rulers and authorities and put them to open
> shame, by triumphing over them in him. (Colossians 2:13–15)

The One who is God even over Leviathan suffered on the cross. He is the God who deals in scars, for he bears them in the person of his Son. When the darkness of Leviathan's presence overwhelms us, we may turn with confidence to this God alone. Shortly after the First World War, at a time when Europe reeled under the burden of unutterable darkness, the poet Edward Shillito wrote a poem that captures something of this truth:

> If we have never sought Thee, we seek Thee now;
> Thine eyes burn through the dark, our only stars;
> We must have sight of thorn-pricks on Thy brow,
> We must have Thee, O Jesus of the Scars.

> The heavens frighten us; they are too calm;
> In all the universe we have no place;
> Our wounds are hurting us; where is the balm?
> Lord Jesus, by Thy Scars, we claim Thy grace.

> The other gods were strong; but Thou wast weak;
> They rode, but Thou didst stumble to a throne;
> But to our wounds only God's wounds can speak,
> And not a god has wounds, but Thou alone.[5]

Notes

1. The poll results were taken from the BBC website in March 2004.
2. Arthur Conan-Doyle, *The Hound of the Baskervilles.*
3. Quoted in Robert S. Fyall, *How Does God Treat his Friends?* (Christian Focus, 1995), p. 117.
4. Robert S. Fyall, *Now My Eyes Have Seen You* (Apollos, 2002), pp. 126–137.
5. Quoted in David Smith, *Mission after Christendom* (London, 2003), p. 31.

11 The end comes at the end
(Job 42:7–17)

The end comes at the end. And this is important. Because although in this short study we have reached the end of the book of Job, in our lives we are not yet at the end. When we wake up in the morning, what do we expect our day to be like? We may of course have expectations for a particular day, the prospect of a good party or apprehension about a visit to the dentist. But in general, what do we expect of a normal day? For a Christian, what ought to be our idea of the normal Christian life? This is important. Because our idea of normality will govern whether we end up delighted or disappointed at the end of the day.

The book of Job ought to shape our expectation of the normal Christian life. We may think that a little perverse, since Job is such an extreme book; but it is not perverse. For although the book of Job paints in primary colours how God treats his friends, and placards before us supremely how he treats a peculiarly blameless believer, nonetheless we have no reason to expect that he will treat us in any radically different way if we belong to Christ.

We left the end of the last chapter at a moment of high drama where the Lord himself spoke to Job. To break off there was a bit like those ice-cream vans that play a part of a tune and then suddenly stop part-way through; and we wait for the end, the resolution, some sense of closure, some rounding off of the tune so that we may relax and go home knowing it is finished.

In Job 42 we have the closure to the story, the resolution, the conclusion, the end. But what are we to make of it? On the face of it, it is a bit of an anticlimax. At least from verse 7 onwards, where it goes back from poetry to prose and frankly it feels a bit prosaic. After the dramatic imagery and the soaring heights of the poetry, it feels a bit of a come down: the Lord has a quiet word of rebuke for the friends (7–9), Job prays for them and they are forgiven. Then it all ends happily, Job is restored to greater prosperity, given a new family and generally rides off into the sunset. Is it not a bit flat, a bit sugary even? And yet there are depths in this conclusion that are neither shallow nor sugary.

This final chapter will be structured around a verse in the letter of James. James is speaking to believers under pressure; he wants them to persevere, and he writes: *Behold, we consider those blessed who remained steadfast. You have heard of the steadfastness of Job, and you have seen the purpose of the Lord, how the Lord is compassionate and merciful* (James 5:11). James focuses on two people: Job with his perseverance and the Lord with his compassion and mercy. Let us begin with Job.

The perseverance of Job

Job's perseverance or steadfastness or patience is an active quality, a pressing on, not a passive sitting back and letting it all wash over me. And there are two aspects of Job's perseverance: perseverance in warfare and perseverance while waiting.

Perseverance in warfare

The book of Job is so refreshingly honest about this. Although Christians sometimes groan at the prospect of studying Job, again and again they are surprised and refreshed by the sheer honesty of this book. We have seen that Job the believer is a battlefield. There is a battle going on; the Lord has been challenged by Satan, Leviathan, a monster masquerading as god. And as they war, it is not so much that Job is on the battlefield; he *is* the battlefield. The battle for the soul of Job is fought out in his struggles as the monster tears at his life. It is a dark warfare. Satan fills Job's mind with images of despair, darkness, death and futility. And Job is taken through the valley of the shadow of death.

He is taken there because he is a believer, suffering for his faith – he is suffering because he is a believer. We saw this in Job 1 and 2: God singles out Job and says, 'Look, there's a believer.' Satan attacks Job for precisely that reason. Job is not about human suffering in general; it is about the suffering endured by a believer because he or she is a believer. Job is being persecuted, not by human enemies but by Satan. He endures disaster, tragedy and sickness, because he fears God.

Supremely, this dark warfare is fulfilled in Jesus Christ. Jesus is the blameless believer. And as we see in the Gospels, Satan focuses his attack on Jesus with an even greater ferocity than upon Job. From Herod's attempt to have him slaughtered as a toddler, through the temptations in the wilderness to the agony of the cross, Satan tears at Jesus' soul – temptation, discouragement, loneliness, betrayal, mis-understanding, agony. Day by day the Lord Jesus awoke to dark warfare.

But if Job is fulfilled in Jesus, every follower of Jesus is called to follow in the footsteps of Job. Job foreshadows Jesus, and the disciple cannot avoid the shadow. As Jesus said to Simon Peter, *Simon, Simon, behold, Satan demanded to have you* [plural]*, that he might sift you like wheat, but I have prayed for you* [singular] *that your faith may not fail* (Luke 22:31–32).

Jesus did not pray that his disciple would be spared the sifting, that Satan would be forbidden his demand. Rather he expected the demand would be granted, as it had been for Job. And he prays that in this painful sifting Simon's faith may not fail. We ought to expect this. Every morning we ought to wake up and say to ourselves, 'There is a vicious dark spiritual battle being waged in me today.' Satan is very busy; wherever on earth there is a believer walking with God in loving fear, God says, 'Look, there's a believer,' and Satan says, 'May I attack him/her? I want to prove whether this is a real believer.' And in one way or another the Lord gives permission. And we ought not to be surprised, as though something strange were happening to us (1 Peter 4:12).

So here is one inescapable element of the normal Christian life: warfare. That expectation relates to our circumstances. The second relates to our attitude of heart.

Perseverance in waiting

Job perseveres by waiting, an active prayer-filled waiting. In Job 42:7 God says to Eliphaz, *you have not spoken of me what is right, as my servant Job has.* Now on the face of it this is a surprising thing for God to say. It is not surprising to us that God says the friends were wrong, but it ought to surprise us that the Lord says that Job is right. For again and again Job says terrible things about God. And yet in spite of the fact that Job charges God with being a wrongdoer (which is both serious and untrue), God can say at the end that Job has spoken rightly of him. How is this?

It is possible that God's affirmation refers only to Job's humble response to God's speeches (40:3–5 and 42:1–6), but it would seem to apply more widely, not only to what Job has said, but to who Job is. The answer would seem to be this: the friends have a theological scheme, a very tidy system, well swept, well defined and entirely satisfying to them. But they have no relationship with the God behind their formulas. There is no wonder, no awe, no longing, no yearning and no prayer to meet and speak with and hear and see the God of their formulas. No, they are content with the rules of the system they have invented.

Now some of their statements considered on their own are correct. For example, in 5:13 Eliphaz says that God *catches the wise in their own craftiness*: the clever person will be caught out by God. That is true, and Paul quotes Eliphaz with approval in 1 Corinthians 3:19. But although the friends make some statements that are true, they do not as a whole speak rightly of God, because they have no relationship with God, no seeking of God and no longing for God. For them he is a dead doctrine and an abstract theory.

But Job does speak rightly. We have seen that it is one of the great motifs of Job's laments that he longs to bring his perplexity to God himself. Job cannot be satisfied with any system: he must know God and speak to the living God. He must, for nothing else will satisfy him. This heart longing of Job is the core reason why the Lord says Job has spoken rightly of him. And of course it leads to Job speaking rightly of the Lord in his humble responses to the Lord's speeches. While the friends want a system, Job wants God. The friends would not have been at church prayer meetings – they had no need. But Job would if he could: *Oh, that I knew where I might find him* (23:3).

The Lord's response to Job is instructive. For in his affirmation of Job, in spite of the terrible things Job says about God, 'We are forcibly reminded that God, for all his rough handling of his servant's rude demands, reads between the lines and listens to the heart.'[1]

We ought to expect that the normal Christian life will be full of unresolved waiting and yearning for God. That is the mark of a believer, of personal religion. So we should never be fatalists. A fatalist looks at circumstances and says, 'What will be, will be.' There is some impersonal power up there sorting it out. Sometimes we Christians say that, but we ought not to. We ought to say, 'What is God doing, the God who is my Maker and my lover? Where is this personal God in all this? If only I could speak to him; if only I might find him.' Such directed, prayer-filled waiting is the integrating arrow of hope that holds together the authentic Christian life.

So we learn from the perseverance of Job that we ought to expect warfare and waiting, struggle and prayer. Now let us move on from the perseverance of Job to the mercy of God.

The compassion and mercy of the Lord

James says, *You have . . . seen the purpose of the Lord, how the Lord is compassionate and merciful* (James 5:11).

Few of us would have described God's behaviour in Job as *compassionate and merciful*. After all, was it not God who gave Satan permission to destroy Job's possessions, to kill Job's children and to ruin Job's health? Yes, it was. The book is quite clear about that. Is that compassion and mercy? Not obviously.

Earlier we considered the analogy of Satan as a fierce dog biting someone, and yet held on a leash by its master. However, in normal life we hold the owner responsible for the violence inflicted by the dog, and the book of Job makes no attempt to dodge this objection. We saw at the start that there is no hesitation both at start and finish in insisting that the Lord alone is the Sovereign God. Satan is not an equal and opposite power, so that God says, 'I'm doing my best to protect you, but I can't win them all.' No, there is no dualism; God is in control and for what happens he is responsible.

So what does James mean when he says, *the Lord is compassionate and merciful?* He says this because of *the purpose of the Lord*, which is to say the end or goal for which God has been working. We see this end in Job 42. Here are three elements from Job 42 of the compassion and mercy of the Lord.

Humbling (42:1–6)

God loves Job enough to humble him. When God speaks, Job responds with few words and silent awe. We see this in 40:4–5 and again in 42:1–6. Job says:

> *Therefore I despise myself,*
> *and repent in dust and ashes.*
> (42:6)

When Job says he repents, it does not mean the friends have been right all along, that Job has secret sins and finally has to admit them and repent. No, he maintains his integrity all along. But he realizes he has been presumptuous: he has (verse 3) spoken of things he does not understand and has overreached himself. Now in the presence of the living God he bows down in silent worship.

And that is a good thing! For Job to be brought low so that he despises himself and exalts God is not a bad thing. We understand that for us to go around thinking we are worms in relation to our fellow human beings is a destructive thing: that kind of inferiority complex, pathological low self-esteem, is not to be encouraged. Better to say, 'I'm OK; you're OK,' as the pop-psychology book had it. But in the presence of the living God, to bow down low and to grasp how great he is and how small I am is a healthy thing. Because it is true. It is a mark of the love of God that he brings Job low, for this is where a creature ought to be.

And it is true for us. We often pray for success, both for us and for others; we pray for good exam results, for good job offers. And yet so often success leads to pride and pride to self-confidence, and self-confidence to independence from God, and independence from God leads to hell. The most deeply compassionate and merciful thing God can do is to humble us and bring us low so that we may bow before him and lean on him and trust him. That is the first mark of the compassion of God: that he loves enough to humble.

And it may be that for some of us there has been or there will be a time in life when everything goes wrong. A time perhaps of pain and failure, even of disaster and misery. And it may be that God in his compassion is bringing us low that we may lean on him alone. This was for Job a hard truth, but it was nonetheless a mark of the mercy of God that he should bring Job very low.

Acceptance (42:7–9)

The technical term is 'justification'. God vindicates Job; he declares him to be in the right. God acknowledges Job as one of his people. We saw earlier how desperately Job longs for this. God does this in three ways:

- In verse 7 he says that Job has spoken rightly of him, whereas the friends have not.
- Repeatedly in verse 7 (once) and verse 8 (twice) God calls Job *my servant* exactly as he did in Job 1 and 2. This is a title of dignity; it is how God characteristically described Moses and the prophets.
- In a nice ironic reversal, the friends are told that Job will pray for them. If we had been Job's friends, we would have been gutted. For we would have expected God to take us on one side and say, 'I want you three, because you are righteous, and the prayer of a righteous man has great power in its effects [James 5:16], to pray for that sinner Job.' But in fact God does the reverse. And this means it is Job who is righteous, justified, vindicated, in right relation with the Lord. For only people right with God can pray and expect their prayers to be answered.

So in these three ways God makes it clear he accepts Job. 'This man is mine; he belongs to me, and I will make sure he is mine for ever.' And this justification, this right relationship with God, is of course what Job has so deeply longed for throughout the drama. It is a mark of the mercy of God that he vindicates Job. And if we are in Christ, God will vindicate us. At the end he will look on each of us and say, 'This one is mine, belongs to me, is my honoured servant.' It is hard to think of a greater mark of God's compassion and mercy than this, however hard the path we tread to get there.

Blessing in the end (42:10–17)

And then, lastly, God blesses Job. The end comes at the end. He gives him greater prosperity (verse 10). He gives him celebration again (verse 11) – this meal being the first celebration since 1:4. Joy comes back into his life. He gives him a new bigger family. He gives him a long life. What are we to make of this?

Let us note that God *first* restored Job to relationship and then blessed him. Job cried out (verse 5) *now my eye sees you* before he was blessed. This is important. Job proves he is a real believer because he bows down to God in a time of pain. It is not that God first blesses him and then Job says, 'You seem to be a good God after all; I will worship you.' No, he worships because God is God and then in the end he is blessed. And when he worships he has no proof or crude certainty that he will be blessed. He lives by faith not by sight.

Also, let us note that the blessing is not a reward for worship. It is not that God says, 'Well done old chap; you've persevered jolly well; now you can have the sweetie I promised you.' Not at all. In fact the doubling of his wealth is a pointer to grace; this is God pouring out undeserved blessing. We must never let the sufferings of Job undermine the grace of God. For God is no man's debtor.

But the most important thing about the blessing is that it happens *at the end*. James understands this perfectly: *Be patient, therefore, brothers,* until the coming of the Lord . . . *You have heard of the steadfastness of Job, and you have seen the purpose of the Lord* . . . (James 5:7, 11; my emphasis).

The purpose of the Lord to show mercy and compassion will be seen finally only when the Lord Jesus returns in glory. Job 42 anticipates the return of the Lord Jesus. The end comes at the end. The normal Christian life is warfare and waiting and being loved and humbled by God, and being justified by God, all in the here and now. But it is the expectation of blessing *at the end*. Often we do get blessed now; we get all sorts of blessing here and now. But the blessings we get now are just a tiny foretaste of the blessings to be poured out at the end.

And the blessings God will pour out on the believer at the end will be every bit as *real* as the blessings of Job. Job knew real prosperity, real joy and celebration, real fruitfulness and real beauty (his dazzling daughters!). The blessings of the new heavens and new earth will be rock solid real; we look forward to beauty that makes the most beautiful woman in the world seem dull; we look forward to fruitfulness that will make the most abundant family in the world seem barren; we look forward to prosperity that will make Bill Gates seem poor; and we look forward to celebration that will make the best party in the world seem like a quiet glass of apple juice.

So as we end this study, let us remember what we ought to expect of the normal Christian life.

- *Warfare.* For each believer is a battlefield and the battle is sometimes dark. Let us be honest about that and not be surprised.
- *Waiting.* We are to be full of prayer, longing, yearning, passionate, even desperate prayer, as we wait for God to act.
- *Humbling.* When we are brought low, it is a mark of God's mercy that we may learn to lean on him alone.
- *Acceptance or justification.* Here and now we may know God has accepted us, and we belong to him forever.
- *Blessing in the end.* For when the Lord returns he will shower such blessing on us that we will not be able to contain it.

This is the message of Job 42 in the Bible.

Notes

1. Derek Kidner, *Wisdom to Live by* (IVP, 1985), p. 73.

Postscript: so what is the book of Job about?

Too often we come to the book of Job (as to other parts of the Bible) expecting answers to our questions. And especially to questions about suffering. The main human character certainly suffers, but the book of Job is not fundamentally about suffering. Job suffers *because he is a believer* and he suffers *as a believer*. And because he is a suffering *believer* the central character and subject of the book of Job is not Job who suffers but the God with whom he has to deal. The book of Job is about God. This ought not to surprise us, but it is easy to forget. If we take our eye off the central focus and major instead on suffering, we shall be disappointed – for we do not find in Job the answers to the questions we have chosen to pose.

Instead we find what Job found when he ultimately had to listen to God: that God asks him questions more than Job poses puzzlers to God. And this turns the tables, as they must be turned. For the book of Job is not about Job, but about God – his character, sovereignty, justice, goodness and, yes, even his love. Above all it is about God the Creator of everything, the God who is God, who made everything, even the wildest corners of the created order, even evil and death. He is the God who made and who entirely controls Leviathan, Satan, the beast and monster who seeks to destroy Job. Even this hideous monster is God's monster, God's creature.

And therefore Job is about true worship, a person bowing down in reality and in the darkness to the God who is God, leaving even our most agonized unanswered questions at his feet. For we are creatures and he alone is the Creator.

Because Job is about God and the worship of God, it is also about humility. Humility to admit (as Job 28 shows) that there is so much about this world that we do not understand. Wisdom with a capital 'W' is God's preserve. It is presumptuous of us to act as if we had made the world, which is what we do the moment we suggest that we could run this world better than God. Humility means to do precisely what Job was doing at the beginning, and what Job 28:28 affirms: to bow before God in loving fear and to turn away from evil. In New Testament terms it is to repent and believe, to hear and to heed the gospel. Here is the gospel in Job, repentance and faith practised at the start, and repentance and faith affirmed at the end.

But of course Job is also about Job. He is the central human character in the drama, introduced at the start and blessed at the end. He is addressed personally by the Lord, where the other human characters are either ignored or rebuked. And so Job points us to the mystery at the heart of the universe, that a blameless believer who walks in fellowship with his Creator, may suffer terrible and undeserved pain, may go through deep darkness and then at the end be vindicated. For there is such a thing in the universe as suffering that is not a punishment for the sin of the sufferer.

And therefore Job is passionately and profoundly about Jesus, whom Job foreshadows both in his blamelessness and in his perseverance through undeserved suffering. As the blameless believer par excellence, Jesus fulfils Job. As a priestly figure who offers sacrifices for his children at the start and his friends at the end, Job foreshadows Jesus the great High Priest. The monstrous ferocity of the beast Leviathan reaches its vicious depths in the life and death of Jesus, who in his passion endures deeper depths and a more solemn and awesome darkness even than Job. The drama, the pain and the perplexity of Job reach their climax at the cross of Jesus Christ. In the darkness and God-forsakenness of those terrible hours of lonely agony, the sufferings of Job are transcended and fulfilled. And as the blameless believer accused and despised by men but finally vindicated by God in the resurrection, Jesus fulfils the drama and longings of Job for justification.

And because Job is about Jesus, it is also, derivatively, about every man and woman in Christ. Every disciple, called to take up the cross and walk in the footsteps of Christ, must expect in some measure to walk also in the footsteps of Job. And so in the end we may conclude that Job is in some measure about us. Not primarily about us, for it is above all about God. Not centrally about us, for its central human character foreshadows Christ. But for each of us as a believer walking through this world in union with Christ, Job is an unavoidable part of the pathway of faith. Our final justification will come through present suffering. Those who today are not recognized as children of God will one day publicly be acknowledged as his (see Romans 8:19). So as we return again and again to this book of Job, and meditate on its depths, let us pray to be given grace to bow down, especially in the darkness, to the God who is God. For it is this God, who is God even of the wild, evil and seemingly random fringes of life, we are called to love and to trust. In the footsteps of the Lord Jesus we too may entrust ourselves to him who judges justly (1 Peter 2:23).

For further study

Job has spawned a vast literature of all kinds. Four of the best recent treatments are as follows:

John E. Hartley, *The Book of Job*, New International Commentary on the Old Testament (Grand Rapids, Mich.: Eerdmans, 1988), is a thorough and comprehensive commentary that addresses all the major issues from a conservative standpoint.

Robert S. Fyall, *How Does God Treat his Friends?* (Christian Focus, 1995), is a short, readable and immensely stimulating book, drawn from talks originally given to the Christian Union at Durham University.

Robert S. Fyall, *Now my Eyes Have Seen you* (Apollos, 2002), is a scholarly work particularly valuable for its treatment of Leviathan and Behemoth.

Norman C. Habel, *The Book of Job* (Philadelphia: Westminster Press, 1985), is a readable commentary especially perceptive in its treatment of the literary structure of Job.